Great Essays

Great Essays

*An Introduction to
Writing Essays*

Keith S. Folse
University of South Florida, Tampa

April Muchmore-Vokoun
University of South Florida, Tampa

Elena Vestri Solomon
University of South Florida, Tampa

Houghton Mifflin Company
Boston New York

Sponsoring Editor: Susan Maguire
Senior Associate Editor: Kathy Sands Boehmer
Editorial Assistant: Kevin M. Evans
Development Editor: Kathleen M. Smith
Project Editor: Kellie Cardone
Senior Production/Design Coordinator: Jill Haber
Senior Manufacturing Coordinator: Priscilla Abreu
Marketing Manager: Patricia Fossi

Cover Designer: Harold Burch Designs, NYC
Cover Image: Harold Burch Designs, NYC
Illustrations: Taz Sibley
Interior Design: Greta D. Sibley & Associates

Printed in the U.S.A.

Library of Congress Catalog Card Number: 98-72027

ISBN: 0-395-90425-0

11 12 13 14 15 16-CS-04 03 02 01

Contents

Part II   Appendices   124

Overview

Great Essays gives introductory instruction and extensive practical exercises and activities in essay writing at the high-intermediate and advanced levels. This book contains a wide variety of exercises that offer practice in both working with the writing process and developing a final written product. We assume that students can write good paragraphs and that what they need is instruction in, modeling of, and guidance with essays.

There are as many ways to write essays as there are writers. Essay writing reflects a writer's knowledge of essay conventions as much as it reflects the writer's creativity. Thus, essay writing is both a science and an art. Since no art form can be "taught" precisely, this book offers models of good academic essays as the basic level of essay writing from which students produce their own essays. We realize that some students may not go beyond the level of the examples whereas other students may advance in their essay writing.

In *Great Essays* we have made a conscious effort to include a wide array of writing activities representing varying approaches to the teaching of writing. Although we realize that few writing teachers are completely satisfied with any writing text, we believe that within this wide variety of activities and approaches, most teachers will find what their students need in order to improve writing skills, presented in a way that is compatible with how teachers think ESL writing ought to be taught.

We have made every effort to include more than enough writing instruction and practice to eliminate the need for excessive ancillary materials. The textbook contains sixty activities with approximately twenty-five suggestions for additional essay writing assignments. In addition, the text has appendices with supplementary practice in language usage and grammar. Most of these activities and practice exercises are based on the twenty-four full-length essays found throughout the text.

We designed this book for high-intermediate to advanced students. Depending on the class level and the amount of writing that is done outside of class hours, there is enough material for sixty to eighty classroom hours. Provided that enough writing is done outside of the classroom, the number of hours can be as little as forty.

Some ESL students are already good writers in their native language. *Great Essays* will allow these students to study the different rhetorical styles commonly used in English writing. Other students need work in the basic steps involved in the process of composing an essay. These students in particular will benefit from the step-by-step activities in *Great Essays*.

Composing an essay involves both a process and a product. All ESL students are rightfully concerned about their written products. For many students, not being able to write effectively and easily in English is a major obstacle to their educational plans. Thus, the quality of any written work is important. To this end, the activities in this book deal with elements that affect the quality of a written product, including grammar, organization, and logic. Though in this text there is information about both process and product in essay writing, it should be noted that the focus is slightly more on the final written product.

The best judge of which units and which activities should be covered with any group of students is always the teacher. It is up to you to gauge the needs of your students and then match these needs with the material in this book.

TEXT ORGANIZATION

Great Essays consists of two parts. The five units in Part I present the features of a good essay and four kinds of essay writing. Part II includes five appendices that contain a description of the steps in the writing process, grammar practice, information about connectors, peer editing sheets, and an answer key.

PART I

Part I begins by teaching, in general terms, how to construct a good essay. The first unit presents the overall organization of an essay. It also offers some specific suggestions for writing the introduction of the essay, including how to write a good hook and a solid thesis statement. Students who are already familiar with the essay form may skip most of the material in Unit 1. Units 2 to 5 teach four different kinds of essays. They are narrative, comparison, cause-effect, and argumentative. These four essay types can be covered in any order.

PART II

Part II consists of five appendices. Appendix 1 explains the seven steps in the process of writing an essay and includes student examples for a few of the steps.

Appendix 2 has additional grammar activities in the context of paragraphs within whole essays. Many ESL students see grammar as their biggest problem. While other writing needs often deserve more attention, students recognize that their ability to express themselves in English is limited by the level of their English proficiency. To help with some of the most common grammar problems, Appendix 2 contains practice exercises.

Appendix 3 contains a list of useful connectors, supplementing the Language Focus sections that feature connectors in the units.

In Appendix 4 you will find peer editing sheets for students to use when they read each other's work and offer feedback. For each essay type, there is a peer editing sheet for the outline and another for the essay. We believe that asking a student to comment on another student's writing without guidance is poor pedagogy and may result in hurt feelings for the writer. Not everyone is a good writer; therefore, we cannot assume that a less capable writer is able to make useful comments on a better writer's paper. Likewise, not all good writers know how to guide weaker writers toward an improved essay. These peer editing sheets provide focused guidance to help everyone make useful comments.

For those students who are able to go beyond the basics, several of the questions are open-ended and invite additional comments.

Finally, Appendix 5 is the answer key to the activities.

CONTENTS OF A UNIT

Following are the common features of each unit. Though each unit has a specific writing goal and language focus (listed at the beginning of the unit), the following features appear in every unit.

EXAMPLE ESSAYS

Because we believe that writing and reading are inextricably related, the example essays are often preceded by short schema-building questions for small groups or the whole class. Potentially unfamiliar vocabulary is underlined in the essay and defined after it. Example essays are usually followed by questions specifically constructed to focus learners' attention on organization, syntactic structures, or other essay features.

WRITER'S NOTES

Rather than large boxed areas overflowing with information, *Great Essays* features small chunks of writing advice under this heading. The content of these notes varies greatly from brainstorming techniques to peer editing guidelines to hints for generating supporting details.

LANGUAGE FOCUS

This section focuses students' attention on word-level details that we believe are important to the kind of essay featured in the unit. If students work with different writing devices, such as connectors, they will be better equipped to use them in their own writing. Those students who need more practice should work through any related additional practices in Appendix 2.

COMPLETING AN OUTLINE

In each unit, students are asked to read partial outlines and fill in the missing pieces. This strategy will help develop students' organizational skills in providing appropriate supporting details and in organizing ideas within an essay.

COMPLETING A SAMPLE ESSAY

In Units 2 to 5, students are asked to fill in the missing supporting details in a partial essay, which is a reinforcement of the model presented earlier in the unit. We designed this activity to give further practice in writing supporting sentences in paragraphs.

ANALYZING AN ESSAY

For each essay type, students using *Great Essays* are asked to read an essay and answer questions that focus on various aspects of writing at the high-intermediate to advanced levels, for example, recognizing the topic sentence, identifying the use of examples as support, or discovering the writer's purpose for including certain information.

TOPICS FOR WRITING

Each unit ends with an assignment to write an essay in the rhetorical style covered in the unit. For further practice, we include a list of five additional writing ideas in each unit.

PEER EDITING

In these activities in each unit, student partners offer each other written comments with the goal of improving their essays. Just as students have different writing abilities, so also do they have different editing abilities. For this reason, we believe that students benefit from *guided* peer editing. After students write an outline, they can use the peer editing sheet for outlines, which addresses content and organization. Students can receive valuable advice from each other regarding thesis statements, topic sentences, supporting information, and logic before writing the essay. The second peer editing activity is for the essay. Pairs of students exchange their completed essays and offer written comments, using the peer editing sheet. We recommend that students spend fifteen to twenty minutes reading a classmate's essay and writing comments according to the questions on the peer editing sheet. Since a certain amount of trust and cooperation is involved in peer editing, it is important to make sure that students work with peers that they feel compatible with.

ABOUT THE ACTIVITIES AND PRACTICES

Teachers have long noticed that students often do well with grammar in discrete sentences but may have problems with the same grammar when it occurs in an essay. Consequently, most of the activities and practices in *Great Essays* work with complete essays or focus on one paragraph within an essay. For example, instead of several unrelated sentences for practice with connectors, there is a complete essay. Our hope is that by practicing the grammatical problem in the target medium, students will produce more accurate writing sooner.

The earliest ESL composition textbooks were merely extensions of ESL grammar classes. The activities in these books did not practice English composition as much as they did ESL grammar points. Later books, on the other hand, tended to focus too much on the composing process. We feel that this focus ignores the important fact that the real goals of our ESL students are both to produce a presentable product and to master the composing process. From our years of ESL and other L2 teaching experience, we believe that *Great Essays* allows ESL students to achieve both of these goals.

ACKNOWLEDGMENTS

We would like to thank ESL and English composition colleagues who generously shared their ideas, insights, and feedback on L2 writing, university English course requirements, and textbook design. In addition, we would like to thank teachers on two electronic lists, TESL-L and TESLIE-L, who responded to our queries and thereby helped us write this book.

We would also like to thank our editors at Houghton Mifflin, Susan Maguire and Kathy Sands Boehmer, and our development editor, Kathleen Smith, for their indispensable guidance throughout the birth and growth of this project.

Likewise, we are indebted to the following reviewers who offered ideas and suggestions that shaped our revisions:

Mathew Clements, California State University, Northridge, CA

Kathy Flynn, Glendale Community College, CA

Norman Prange, Cuyahoga Community College, OH

Charlotte Calobisi, Northern Virginia Community College, VA

Colleen Weldele, Palomar College, CA

Finally, many thanks go to our students who have taught us what ESL composition ought to be. Without them, this work would have been impossible.

Keith S. Folse
April Muchmore-Vokoun
Elena Vestri Solomon

Part I

Essays

Unit 5   Argumentative Essays

Unit I

Exploring the Essay

GOAL: To learn about the structure of an essay

WHAT IS AN ESSAY?

Essays are everywhere—in books, magazines, newspapers, and other printed material. An essay is a short collection of paragraphs that presents facts, opinions, and ideas on a topic. Topics can range from a description of a visit to Disney World to an argument about capital punishment.

An essay usually has three to ten paragraphs. Most of the essays in this book have five or six paragraphs. Each paragraph discusses one idea, often stated in the topic sentence of the paragraph. This idea is related to the topic of the whole essay. The topic sentence of a paragraph can be located anywhere, but the most common place is at the beginning of the paragraph.

The following illustration shows how letters, words, sentences, paragraphs, and essays are related. Letters can be combined into a word. Words can be combined into a sentence. Sentences can be combined into a paragraph. Finally, paragraphs can be combined into an essay. In this book, you will study essays.

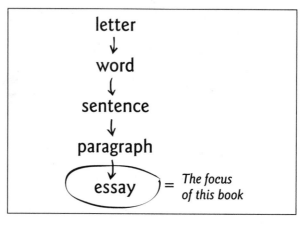

Connections

KINDS OF ESSAYS

There are many different ways to write an essay. The method that a writer chooses is based on the topic of the essay and the kind of essay that presents the topic in the best way. For example, in an essay that compares Civil War weapons with World War II weapons, the writer would use a comparison format.

In this book, you will learn about four common kinds of essays: narrative, comparison, cause-effect, and argumentative. Each of the next four units presents one of these kinds of essay writing. However, it is important to note here that most writers use more than one method. For example, if you are contrasting Civil War weapons with World War II weapons, you might include information about what caused the weapons technology to be developed (cause-effect). You might also give an account of how this technology was manufactured in a specific factory (narrative). In addition, your essay could include facts and opinions about how one kind of weapon was more effective than another (argumentative).

It is likely that a good writer will use more than one kind of writing in an essay. Once you learn about these essay methods separately and become comfortable with them, you can experiment with weaving them together to produce well-written essays in English.

WRITER'S NOTE: Parts of an Essay

Notice that an essay always has three basic parts: the **introduction,** the **body,** and the **conclusion.** The introduction is the first paragraph, the conclusion is the last paragraph, and the body consists of the paragraphs in between. You will study these three parts later in this unit.

EXAMPLE ESSAYS

Read and study these five example essays. Work with a partner to answer the questions before and after the essays. These questions will help you understand the content and the organization of the essays.

Activity 1   Studying an Example Essay

Essay 1

This essay is about typical household chores and what the writer thinks about them.

1. How much time do you spend cleaning your house or apartment each week?
2. What is your least favorite household chore? Why?

Cinderella and Her <u>Odious</u> <u>Household</u> <u>Chores</u>

1   Everyone knows how the story of Cinderella ends, but did you ever really think about how she spent her days before she met the prince? Her daily routine was not glamorous. She did everything from sweeping the floor to cooking the meals. If someone had asked Cinderella, "Are there any household chores that you particularly hate?" she probably would have answered, "Why, none, of course. Housework is my duty!" In the real world, however, most people have definite dislikes for certain household chores. The top three of these tasks include ironing clothes, washing dishes, and cleaning the bathroom.

2   One of the most hated chores for many people is ironing clothes because it is not a task that can be completed quickly or thoughtlessly. Each piece of clothing must be handled individually, so ironing a basket of laundry can take hours! After ironing a piece of clothing <u>meticulously</u>, which entails smoothing out the fabric, following the seams, and getting the creases "just right," you need to place it on a hanger as soon as possible. If you do not follow these directions carefully, it might become wrinkled and you have to start over. Perhaps that is why ironing is not a favorite chore. It requires extreme attention to detail from beginning to end.

3   Another household chore that many people dislike is washing dishes. Of course, some people claim that this chore is no longer a problem because we have dishwashers now! However, no one would argue that dishes, <u>silverware</u>, and especially pots and pans washed in a dishwasher come out as clean as they do when washed by hand. For this reason, many of us continue to wash our dishes by hand, but we are not necessarily happy doing it. Washing dishes is a dirty job that requires not only the <u>elbow grease</u> to scrape food off the dishes but also the patience to rinse and dry them. In addition, unlike ironing clothes, washing dishes is a chore that usually must be done every day. I don't know how Cinderella felt about this particular chore, but I believe that most people hate it as much as I do.

4   Though ironing clothes and washing dishes are not the most pleasant household chores, perhaps the most dreaded is cleaning the bathroom. This involves <u>tackling</u> three main areas: the bathtub, sink, and toilet. Because the bathroom is full of germs, a quick wiping of the surfaces is not enough. As a result, you must use strong bathroom cleansers to clean and <u>disinfect</u> this room. The task of cleaning the bathroom is so unpleasant that some people wear rubber gloves when they attempt it. The only positive point about cleaning the bathroom is that it does not have to be done on a daily basis.

ESSAY **5** Maintaining a house means doing a wide variety of unpleasant chores. Cinderella knew this, and so do we. Many of us do not have the luxury of hiring an outside person to do our housework, so we must make do with our responsibilities. If we can take pride in the results of our hard work, maybe we can get through the unpleasantness of these typical household chores.

odious: very unpleasant

household: referring to the house

chore: a specific task or job

meticulously: thoroughly and carefully

silverware: eating utensils; forks, knives, and spoons

elbow grease: physical strength, usually using the hands

tackling: undertaking, beginning

disinfect: purify; eliminate germs

3. According to the author of this essay, what are the three least popular household chores?

_____   _____   _____

WRITER'S NOTE: The Hook

The opening sentence of any essay is called the **hook.** A hook in writing is used to "catch" readers and get their interest so that they will want to read the essay. (See pages 23–24 for more information about hooks.)

4. Write the hook in this essay. _____

_____

5. Do you think this hook is effective? Does it grab your attention? Why, or why not?

_____

_____

6. How many paragraphs does this essay have? _____ Which paragraph is the introduction?

_____ the conclusion? _____ Which paragraphs are the body? _____

7. In a few words, what is the general topic of this essay? _____

8. Can you find a sentence in paragraph 1 that tells readers what to expect in paragraphs 2, 3, and 4?

Write that sentence here. _____

_____

WRITER'S NOTE: The Thesis Statement

In "Cinderella and Her Odious Household Chores," the last sentence in paragraph 1 is the **thesis statement.** It states the main idea of the essay and tells what the organization of the information will be. (See pages 25–26 for more information about thesis statements.)

9. What is the topic of paragraph 2? _____

Can you find one sentence that introduces this topic? Write it here.

_____

_____

_____

WRITER'S NOTE: The Topic Sentence

Every good paragraph has a **topic sentence.** The topic sentence tells the reader the main topic of the paragraph. Sometimes it also gives the reader a hint about the writer's purpose.

10. Write the topic sentences of paragraph 3 and paragraph 4.

Paragraph 3: _____

_____

_____

_____

Paragraph 4: _____

_____

_____

_____

WRITER'S NOTE: Supporting Sentences

The **supporting sentences** in an essay are in the body. (See pages 31–36 for information about the body.) Supporting sentences always relate to the topic sentence of the paragraph in which they occur. Common supporting sentences give examples, reasons, facts, or more specific information. Without supporting sentences, an essay would be nothing more than a general outline.

11. Supporting sentences: In paragraph 2, the writer shows that people do not like to iron clothes. Write two of the supporting sentences here.

_____

_____

_____

12. Supporting sentences: In paragraph 4, the writer suggests that cleaning the bathroom is not a simple or fast chore. Write the sentence in which the writer makes this point.

_____

_____

_____

13. Look at the last paragraph. Find the sentence that restates the thesis. Write that sentence here.

_____

_____

_____

WRITER'S NOTE: The Conclusion

It is important for an essay to have a good **conclusion.** Notice that the writer mentions Cinderella again in the last paragraph of "Cinderella and Her Odious Household Chores." The introduction and the conclusion often share some ideas and words. (See pages 36–37 for more information about writing the conclusion of an essay.)

Activity 2   **Studying an Example Essay**

Essay 2

In this narrative essay, the narrator experiences a humorous language problem in Japan.

1. What are some words that cause problems for you in English? Why are they difficult?

2. Describe a situation in which you could not express yourself effectively in English. What did you do?

EXAMPLE ESSAY

How Do You Say . . . ?

1   What would happen if you woke up one day and suddenly found yourself in a world where you could not communicate with anyone? I am a teacher of English as a second language (ESL). In June 1988, I accepted a job in a <u>rural</u> area of Japan called Niigata and found myself faced with this language problem. One event <u>in particular</u> <u>stands out</u> as an example of my inability to express my ideas to the people around me <u>due to</u> my <u>lack</u> of vocabulary.

2   I had been in Japan only a few days, and I was feeling restless. I wanted to make some fresh bread, so I <u>set out for</u> the store with the simple intention of buying some flour. I had taken some Japanese language classes before I arrived in Japan. Although I knew my Japanese skills were limited, my lack of knowledge did not stop me from going to the store to buy flour. I thought that I would locate the section where the grains were displayed and find the bag that had a picture of either bread or flour on it.

3   The small town where I lived had one tiny store. I wandered around the store a few times, but I did not see a bag of anything that appeared to be flour. In the United States, flour usually comes in a paper bag with pictures of biscuits or bread on it, so this is what I was looking for. I finally found a few clear plastic bags that had bread <u>crumbs</u> inside, so I thought that flour might be located nearby. No matter how many bags I examined, I could not find any flour.

4   I desperately wanted to ask one of the three elderly women clerks where the flour was, but I could not do this simple task. I knew how to ask where something was, but I did not know the word for "flour." I tried to think of how to say "flour" using different words such as "white powder" or "the ingredient that you use to make bread," but I did not know "powder" and I did not know "ingredient." Just then, I saw one of my students leaving the store. I rushed outside to his car and explained that I needed to know a word in Japanese. "How do you say 'flour'?" I asked. He told me the word was *hana*.

5   I rushed back into the store, which was about to close for the evening. I found one of the elderly clerks and asked in my best Japanese, *"Sumimasen. Hana wa doko desu ka?"* or "Excuse me. Where is the *hana*?" The petite old woman said something in Japanese and raced to the far right side of the store. "Finally," I thought, "I'm going to get

EXAMPLE ESSAY

my flour and go home to make bread." However, my hopes ended rather quickly when I followed the clerk to the <u>produce</u> section. I saw green onions, tomatoes, and even <u>pumpkins</u>, but I could not understand why flour would be there. The woman then pointed to the beautiful yellow <u>chrysanthemums</u> next to the green onions.

6 At first I was puzzled, but suddenly it all made sense. I had been in the country long enough to know that people in Japan eat chrysanthemums in salads. I was standing in front of the f-l-o-w-e-r display, not the f-l-o-u-r display. When I asked my student for the Japanese word for "flour," I did not <u>specify</u> whether I meant "flour" or "flower" because it had never occurred to me that grocery stores, especially small ones, might sell flowers.

7 I did not buy any chrysanthemums that night. I was not able to find the flour either. My lack of knowledge about Japanese cuisine and my very limited knowledge of Japanese caused me to go home empty-handed that night. However, I learned the often-underestimated value of simple vocabulary in speaking a second language. For me, this event in a small store in rural Japan really opened my eyes to my lack of vocabulary skills.

rural: of the countryside; the opposite of *urban*

in particular: especially

stand out: to be different from the other members of the group

due to: because of

lack: a shortage

set out for: to start going to a place

crumbs: tiny pieces of food

produce: fresh fruits and vegetables

pumpkin: a large, round, orange fruit

chrysanthemum: a type of flower

specify: to say exactly

3. In a few sentences, tell what happened in this story. Use your own words.

_____

_____

_____

_____

_____

_____

4. A good hook in an essay sometimes involves the reader in what follows. Write the hook for this essay.

_____

_____

5. How does this hook try to involve the reader? Do you think that this hook is successful? Why, or why not?

   _____

   _____

   _____

6. How many paragraphs are in this essay? _____ In which paragraph does the writer

   reveal what the problem is with the question he asked in Japanese? _____

7. Supporting sentences: Why does the writer include the information in paragraph 6? (Hint: What supporting information does the writer give to explain the language miscommunication?)

   _____

   _____

8. This essay tells a story. It is an organized sequence of events. This kind of essay is called a **narrative essay** (Unit 2).

   Here is a list of the main events in the essay. Read the list and number the items from 1 to 12 to indicate the order of the events.

   _____ The clerk took the writer to the produce section.

   _____ The writer asked the student for a Japanese translation.

   _____ The clerk pointed to the flowers.

   _____ The writer arrived in Japan.

   _____ The writer wanted to make some bread.

   _____ The writer spoke to an elderly clerk.

   _____ The writer realized that the student had not understood the question correctly.

   _____ The writer went home without the flour.

   _____ The writer looked all over the store for the flour.

   _____ The writer saw one of his students.

   _____ The writer studied Japanese.

   _____ The writer went to the store.

| Activity 3 | Studying an Example Essay |

Essay 3

Which do you like better, the city or the countryside? Read this comparison essay about some differences between these two types of places.

1. Describe the place where you grew up.

2. What were the best and worst things about living there?

Differences in <u>Urban</u> and Rural Life

1   Imagine life in Toronto. Now imagine life in a neighboring rural Canadian town. Finally, picture life in Rome, Italy. Which of these last two places is more different from Toronto? Many people might mistakenly choose Rome because it is in a different country. In fact, city <u>dwellers</u> all over the world tend to have similar lifestyles, so the biggest differences are between Toronto and its smaller neighbor. Urban people and rural people, <u>regardless of</u> their country, live quite differently. Perhaps some of the most <u>notable</u> differences in the lives of these two groups include <u>degree</u> of friendliness, <u>pace</u> of life, and variety of activities.

2   One major difference between growing up in the city and in the country is the degree of friendliness. In large cities, we often hear of people living in huge apartment buildings with hundreds of strangers. These urban apartment dwellers tend to be <u>wary</u> of unknown faces and rarely get to know their neighbors well. The situation in a small town is often just the opposite. Small-town people generally grow up together, attend the same schools and churches, and share the same friends. As a result, rural people are much more likely to treat their neighbors like family and invite them into their homes.

3   Another difference is the pace of life. In the city, life moves very quickly. The streets reflect this hectic pace and are rarely empty, even late at night. City dwellers appear to be racing to get somewhere important. Life for them tends to be a series of <u>deadlines</u>. In the country, life is much slower. Even during <u>peak</u> hours, traffic jams occur less often. Stores close in the early evening, and the streets don't come alive until the next morning. The people here seem more relaxed and move in a more leisurely way. The pace of life in these two areas couldn't be more different.

4   A third difference lies in the way people are able to spend their free time. Although life in the city has its <u>drawbacks</u>, city dwellers have a much wider choice of activities that they can participate in. For example, they can go to museums, eat in exotic restaurants, attend concerts, and shop in hundreds of stores. The activities available to people in rural areas, however, are much more limited. It is rare to find museums or exotic restaurants there. Concert tours almost never include stops in country towns. Finally, people who enjoy shopping might be disappointed in the small number of stores.

5   Life in urban areas and life in rural areas vary in terms of human interaction, pace of life, and daily activities. Other important differences exist, too, but none of these makes one place better than the other. The places are simply different. Only people who have experienced living in both the city and the country can truly appreciate the unique characteristics of each.

urban: of the city

dwellers: those who live in a place

regardless of: in spite of

notable: important; worthy of notice

degree: amount

pace: speed; rate

wary: cautious, suspicious

deadline: the time limit for doing something

peak: the highest; the top (amount)

drawbacks: disadvantages, negative points

3. What is the topic of this essay?

The writer's purpose is to compare and contrast life in two locations. This kind of essay is called a **comparison essay** (Unit 3).

4. What is the thesis statement? _____

    _____

    _____

5. In each paragraph, which location is always discussed first, rural or urban?

    _____

6. Which paragraph talks about activities in each area? _____ Which place offers more

    options for activities? _____

7. Supporting sentences: Some of the supporting sentences in "Differences in Urban and Rural Life" contrast the pace of life in the two areas. Write those sentences in the chart under the correct heading. Include the paragraph number.

    _____
    Pace of Life (paragraph _____) _____

    A. Urban

        1. _____

        2. _____

        3. _____

        4. _____

    B. Rural

        1. _____

        2. _____

        3. _____

        4. _____

Activity 4	Studying an Example Essay

Essay 4

This cause-effect essay tells about the connection between cancer and an unhealthy lifestyle.

1. Do you think people are healthier now than in the past? Why, or why not?
2. What three changes could you make in your lifestyle to become healthier? Be specific.

Cancer Risks

EXAMPLE ESSAY

1   Lung cancer kills more people in one year than all criminal and accidental deaths combined. These statistics are shocking, but the good news is that people are now well-informed about the risks connected to lung cancer. They know that their risk of contracting this terrible disease decreases if they either stop smoking or don't smoke at all. Unfortunately, the same cannot be said about other types of cancer. Many people are not aware that their everyday behavior can lead to the development of these different forms of cancer. By eating better, exercising regularly, and staying out of the sun, people can reduce their risks.

2   Instead of foods that are good for them, people often eat hamburgers, cheese, French fries, and pizza. These common foods contain large amounts of saturated fat, which is the worst kind of fat. Though light and fat-free products are constantly being introduced to the consumer market, many people still buy food that contains fat because it often tastes better. However, eating fatty foods can increase a person's chances for some kinds of cancer. People do not eat as many fresh vegetables and fresh fruit as they used to. Instead, they now eat a lot more processed foods that do not contain natural <u>fiber</u>. Lack of fiber in a person's diet can increase the chance of <u>colon</u> cancer. In the past, people with less information about nutrition actually had better <u>diets</u> than people do today. They also had fewer cases of cancer.

3   Many people today are overweight, and being overweight has been connected to some kinds of cancer. This is the generation that started the couch potato boom, and today's couch potatoes are bigger than ever. Health experts warn that being overweight is a risk not only for heart disease but also for certain kinds of cancer. The best way to <u>attain</u> a healthy weight again is to <u>cut back on</u> the amount of food and to exercise regularly. It is not possible to do only one of these and lose weight permanently. The improved diet must be <u>in conjunction with</u> regular exercise. In the past, people did more physical activity than people do today. For example, people used to walk to work; now almost no one does. In addition, people had jobs that required more physical labor. Now many people have desk jobs in front of computers.

4   Finally, health officials are gravely concerned by the <u>astounding</u> rise in the cases of skin cancer. Many societies value a tanned complexion, so on weekends people tend to <u>flock to</u> the beach or swimming pools and lie in the sun. Many of these people don't use a safe sunscreen, and the result is that they often get sunburned. Sunburn damages the skin, and repeated damage may lead to skin cancer later in life. Once the damage is done, it cannot be undone. Thus, prevention is important. In the past, people did not lie in direct sunlight for long periods, and skin cancer was not as <u>prevalent</u> as it is now. People have started to listen to doctors' warnings about this situation, and more and more people are using proper sunscreens. Unfortunately, millions of people already have this potential cancer problem in their skin and may develop cancer later.

5   Cancer has been around since the earliest days of human existence, but only recently has the public been made aware of some of the risk factors involved. Anti-smoking campaigns can be seen everywhere: on billboards, television, radio, and newsprint. If the same amount of attention were given to proper diets, exercise, and sunscreens, perhaps the number of overall cancer cases would be reduced.

fiber: a plant material that is good for the digestive system

colon: an organ in the digestive system

diet: a special plan for losing weight; what a person eats

attain: to achieve

cut back on: to reduce the amount (of something)

in conjunction with: at the same time as; together with

astounding: amazing; surprising

flock to: to go to a place in large numbers (as birds do)

prevalent: common

3. What is the writer's main message in this essay? _____

_____

_____

4. In a few words, what is the general topic of "Cancer Risks"?

_____

The writer presents several causes for the rise in the number of cancer cases. This kind of organization is called a **cause-effect essay** (Unit 4). In this kind of essay, the writer shows that one thing happened (effect) because something else happened first (cause).

5. What is the thesis statement of the essay?

_____

_____

6. The thesis statement should tell the reader how the paper will be organized. What do you know about the organization of the essay from the thesis statement?

_____

_____

7. Supporting sentences: In paragraph 2, the writer states that many people eat unhealthy food. What supporting information explains why this food is not healthy?

_____

_____

8. Supporting sentences: The writer also explains why people enjoy eating unhealthy food. Write the reason here.

_____

_____

| Activity 5 | **Studying an Example Essay** |

Essay 5

Choosing a college is an important decision. This essay may help you decide.

1. What do you know about community colleges? How are they different from universities?

2. What are some things that students consider when they are choosing a college?

The Advantages of Community Colleges

1 A high school diploma is not the end of many people's education these days. High school students who want to continue their education generally choose one of two routes after graduation. Some students <u>opt to</u> attend a community college and then transfer to a university, while others go directly to a university. Making this difficult choice requires a great deal of careful thought. However, if the choice is based on three specific factors, <u>namely</u>, cost, location, and quality of education, students will quickly see the advantages that attending a community college offers.

2 Attending a community college is much cheaper than attending a university. For example, <u>tuition</u> at a local community college I attended might cost less than $3,000 for two years. The same classes taken at a nearby university would cost almost $5,000. In addition, a university would charge more for parking, photocopying at the library, cafeteria food, campus health clinic services, and textbooks. No matter how the total bill is calculated or what is included, it is more expensive to study at a university.

3 Attending a community college can be more convenient because of its location. Going to a university often requires recent high school graduates to live far from home, and many of them are <u>reluctant</u> to do so. These students are only seventeen or eighteen years old and may have very little experience at being away from home. It would be difficult for these young people to suddenly find themselves far away from their families. In addition, very few parents are prepared to send their teenagers to distant universities. Because almost every area has a community college, students who opt to go to a community college can continue to be near their families for two more years.

4 Finally, there are educational benefits to attending a community college. University life is very different from community college life. A university campus offers a large variety of sports events and parties, and students can easily become distracted from their studies. Community colleges, which typically have fewer students and extracurricular activities, may be a better environment for serious study. In addition, the library facilities at a community college, though not as large as those at a university, are more than sufficient for the kind of work that is required in first- or second-year courses. Class size is also an issue to consider. Introductory courses at universities often have fifty to sixty or even one hundred students. In such large classes, student-teacher interaction usually is <u>minimal</u>, and learning can be more difficult for some students. Finally, the teaching at community colleges is often better than the teaching at a university. Professors at community colleges have the same <u>credentials</u> as those at universities, and community college professors spend most of their time teaching instead of conducting research, as university professors have to do.

5 The decision to enter a university directly or to attend a community college for the first two years after high school can be difficult. However, based on the three important factors discussed in this essay—cost, location, and quality of education—it is clear that attending a community college is the smarter thing to do.

opt to: to choose to (do something)

namely: such as; for example

tuition: money paid for classes

reluctant: hesitant

minimal: the least possible

credentials: qualifications

3. What two things are being compared in this essay?

_____

Which one does the writer think is better?

_____

In essays like this one, the writer is comparing or contrasting two or more things. However, unlike "Differences in Urban and Rural Life" (Essay 3, page 14), in "The Advantages of Community Colleges," the writer compares community colleges and universities with the intention of persuading the reader to agree that community colleges are better for new high school graduates. This kind of essay is called an **argumentative essay** (Unit 5). Some books call this a persuasive essay.

4. What is the organization of this essay? Fill in the blanks of this simple outline with the words that are missing.

TOPIC: The Advantages of Community Colleges

Paragraph 1: Introduction

Thesis statement: _____

_____

Paragraph 2 topic: _____

> A. Community college cost: $ _____
>
> B. _____ : $ _____
>
> C. Other higher university costs
>
>   1. Parking
>
>   2. _____
>
>   3. _____
>
>   4. Health clinic services
>
>   5. _____

SUPPORT

Paragraph 3 topic: Location

SUPPORT

A. Students' reasons

B. _____

_____

Paragraph 4 topic: _____

SUPPORT

A. Quiet campus

B. _____

C. Class size

D. Quality of teaching

Paragraph 5: Conclusion

5. The writer discusses three factors—cost, location, and quality of education—in the decision about what kind of college to attend. Can you think of two other factors that the writer could have used?

   _____

   _____

6. Before you read this essay, did you know much about this topic? What was your opinion before you read this essay? (Check all possible answers.)

   _____ I thought that attending a university directly after high school was best.

   _____ I thought that attending a community college after high school was best.

   _____ I thought that a university offered a better education than a community college.

   _____ I thought that a community college offered a better education than a university.

   _____ I thought that a university was cheaper than a community college.

   _____ I thought that a community college was cheaper than a university.

   _____ I did not know much about university education in the United States.

   _____ I did not know much about community college education in the United States.

7. Did your opinion about community colleges change after you read "The Advantages of Community Colleges"? In other words, did the writer persuade you to change your mind about community colleges in the United States? _____

8. Which part of the essay was the most persuasive for you?

_____

_____

9. If your answer to question 7 is "yes," tell why your opinion changed. If your answer to question 7 is "no," can you think of some fact or information that the writer could have used to make the essay more persuasive?

_____

_____

_____

_____

WRITING THE INTRODUCTION

The introduction is the first part of an essay, usually the first paragraph. The introduction does not have to be written first, however. Some writers design and write this part last or at another point in their writing process.

From the basic outline that follows, you can see how the introduction fits into the essay. In this unit, you will learn about the introduction.

I. Introduction (usually one paragraph)
II. Body (one to four paragraphs)
III. Conclusion (usually one paragraph)

There are many ways to write an introduction. Some writers begin with a question. Other writers give background information about the topic. The kind of introduction you choose depends on how you want to present the topic and the kind of essay you decide to write.

WHAT IS IN THE INTRODUCTION?

The introduction for most essays is one paragraph. This introductory paragraph usually consists of three parts:

INTRODUCTION = $\begin{cases} 1. \text{ the hook} \\ 2. \text{ connecting information} \\ 3. \text{ the thesis statement (or writing plan).} \end{cases}$

Now look at each of these parts to see what they are and how they work in the introduction.

The Hook

The hook is the opening statement or statements. Just as a fisherman uses a hook to catch a fish, so a writer uses a hook to catch readers' attention. If a hook does its job well, readers will want to read the rest of the essay after they have read the hook. Writing a good hook is not easy. It requires a great deal of thought and practice.

There are many different ways to write a hook.

1. One common way to write a hook is to ask a question. If readers want to know the answer to the question, they are "hooked" and will read the essay. For example, a writer might begin an essay with this sentence:

> How many people out there on the roads are driving uninsured vehicles?

Most readers won't know the answer to this question, but they'll probably be hooked and want to find out more about the topic.

2. Another way to write a hook is to begin an essay with an interesting observation. Here is an example:

> Asian economists are not sleeping well these days.

This observation makes readers want to know why economists are not sleeping well. To find out, they read on.

Here's another example of an observation hook full of interesting details that leads readers to the subject of international trade:

> The average American is proud to be American, and he is eager to talk about American products. However, the average American drives a Japanese or German car to work every morning. He wears cotton shirts made in Honduras and pants made in Bangladesh. His dinner salad has tomatoes from Mexico and salad dressing from France. Before he goes to bed, he will watch his favorite program on a Japanese television set.

3. Writers often begin an essay with a unique scenario to catch readers' attention:

> Traveling at more than one hundred miles an hour, he feels as though he is not moving. He is engulfed in complete silence. For a moment, it is as if he has entered another dimension.

Are you hooked? Do you want to read the rest of the essay? This essay is about the exciting sport of skydiving.

4. Sometimes writers use a famous quote as a hook, as in this example:

> "To be or not to be; that is the question."

Many readers may think that this hook will lead into a discussion of Shakespeare or the story of *Hamlet*. In fact, this hook begins an essay on the topic of suicide.

WRITER'S NOTE: Hook versus Main Idea

In English writing, the main idea, or thesis, of an essay is usually in the introduction, but it's not often the first sentence. (The hook is usually the first sentence.) If you begin an essay with a sentence stating the main idea, such as:

This essay will talk about the most embarrassing day of my life.

or

There are three ways to curb teen pregnancy.

your readers may not be interested in reading the rest of your essay. These sentences do not grab your readers' attention. Be sure to write a hook and put it first.

Connecting Information

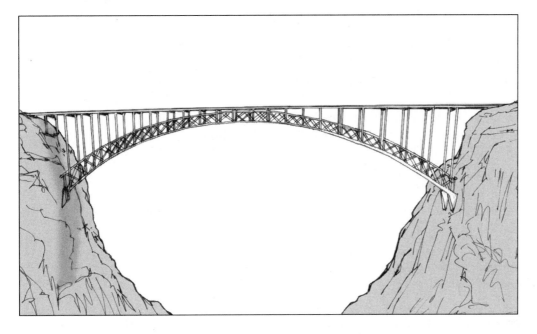

After the hook, the writer usually writes three to five sentences that help connect the reader and the topic. These sentences can be background information about the topic or they can be examples. The following sentences from Essay 1 on page 6 give examples of how Cinderella probably spent her days before she met the prince:

> Her daily routine was not glamorous. She did everything from sweeping the floors to cooking the meals. If someone had asked Cinderella, "Are there any household chores that you particularly hate?" she probably would have answered, "Why, none, of course. Housework is my duty!"

From these sentences, the reader has a good idea of what the topic might be: unpleasant household chores.

WRITER'S NOTE: What Does the Reader Know?

A good writer does not jump into a topic too quickly. First, a good writer tries to imagine what the reader already knows about the topic. Then the writer can focus on bridging the gap between what the reader knows and what he or she needs to know about the topic.

The Thesis Statement

The thesis statement, or writing plan, is usually the last part of the introduction. It can be one or two sentences long. In the thesis statement, the writer tells the reader what to expect in the essay. Basically, there are two kinds of thesis statements, direct and indirect.

Direct Thesis Statement Some writers want to give a specific outline of the paper in their thesis statement. For example:

> The main problems facing South American countries are a lack of job opportunities for citizens, increasing demand for better health care, and limited university programs for poor students.

From this statement, the reader knows that the body of the essay has three main parts. One part will discuss job opportunities, another part will talk about health care needs, and the last part will talk about university programs for poor students. This kind of thesis statement is called a *direct thesis statement*.

Indirect Thesis Statement Other writers are not so direct. On the same topic as the previous example, these writers might use this statement:

> The important problems facing South American countries today require immediate attention.

From this statement, the reader expects to find a discussion of problems in South America. The reader does not know exactly what to expect, but that is not a problem. This kind of thesis statement is called an *indirect thesis statement*.

Both direct and indirect thesis statements are acceptable. It is up to the writer to decide which approach to take.

PRACTICE WITH HOOKS AND THESIS STATEMENTS

The following activities will give you practice writing hooks. You will also compare your hooks with those your classmates wrote. This will help you improve your understanding of how hooks work in essay introductions. Be prepared to explain why you think your hook will attract readers' attention and make them want to read the essay. You will also practice writing and identifying thesis statements.

Activity 6   Practice with Hooks

1. This essay begins with the second sentence. Read the whole essay. Then write three possible hooks on the lines.

Essay 6

In this argumentative essay, the writer argues that mandatory retirement should be abolished.

Mandatory Retirement Has to Go

EXAMPLE ESSAY

1

Hook 1: _____

_____

Hook 2: _____

_____

Hook 3: _____

_____

Traditionally, people retire from their jobs when they reach the age of sixty-five. In some jobs, this is not an option but a requirement. I object to mandatory retirement for capable workers because it violates personal choice, discriminates against senior citizens, and wastes valuable skills as well as money.

2   First of all, I believe that mandatory retirement violates an individual's personal choice of continuing to work or retiring. The older working person should have the right to choose his or her retirement age. A person's right to life, liberty, and the pursuit of happiness (as written in the Declaration of Independence) is a very special thing. Forced retirement takes away people's livelihood, deprives them of their freedom to choose their line of work, and prevents them from pursuing happiness.

3   Second, mandatory retirement is surely a form of age discrimination. A young person might wonder why an older worker should be kept on the payroll when the company

EXAMPLE ESSAY

could hire someone who is younger and more creative. However, a younger person will not necessarily be a better or more creative worker. Age does not indicate the quality of a person's work. Many well-known artists, politicians, and writers developed their best works after the age of sixty. The common belief that a person's mind slows down after a certain age is nothing but a misconception.

4 In addition to the previous two points, there is the issue of quality of work. Older employees have knowledge and experience that can truly be beneficial. Unfortunately, many employers disregard this fact. Captain Al Haynes, age fifty-eight, was able to land a DC-10 that was out of control so that 186 of the 296 people aboard survived when it crashed. McDonald-Douglas, the maker of the DC-10, simulated the same problem forty-five times and not one time did they have a successful landing. Safety experts agree that the high survival rate among the passengers on the flight was due to Captain Haynes's aviation skills. It is doubtful that a less experienced pilot could have accomplished this feat. However, a year later, Captain Haynes had to retire because he had reached the age of sixty, the mandatory retirement age for pilots in the United States.

5 Many people, especially fresh college graduates, do not agree that retirement should be an option. They are worried that if older workers are allowed to continue in their jobs, there will not be enough openings for younger people. However, is there really a danger that older people will take away job opportunities from younger people? This is unlikely because younger workers and older workers rarely compete for the same jobs. In fact, older workers rarely seek entry-level positions. This type of faulty logic was used in the 1960s to oppose the passage of the civil rights laws that now protect women and minorities from employment discrimination. More importantly, the U.S. Department of Labor is concerned that labor shortages might occur when "baby boomers" retire after the year 2000. Therefore, employers should start looking for ways to attract experienced workers, not retire them.

6 In conclusion, the age of retirement should be decided by an individual's economic need, health status, and work preference. Our lives are our own, and we should be allowed to live our lives to the fullest potential. Without a doubt, mandatory retirement goes against fulfilling this potential and should not be a part of modern society.

2. In pairs or small groups, share the three hooks that you wrote with your classmates. Are any of them similar? Explain why you think your hooks will grab readers' attention.

| Activity 7 | Thesis Statement Questions |

Answer these questions about the thesis statement in "Mandatory Retirement Has to Go."

1. What is the thesis statement in the essay?

_____

_____

2. Is this a direct or indirect thesis statement? _____

   Give the reason for your answer. _____

   _____

3. Rewrite the thesis statement as an indirect thesis statement.

   _____

   _____

| Activity 8 | More Practice with Hooks |

1. This essay begins with the second sentence. Read the whole essay. Then write three possible hooks on the lines.

Essay 7

This comparison essay gives facts about education in South Korea and North America.

Differences in Education in South Korea and North America

EXAMPLE ESSAY

Hook 1: _____

_____

Hook 2: _____

_____

Hook 3: _____

_____

The school systems of South Korea, Canada, and the United States are about the same in two areas: the age when students start school and the number of years they go to school. However, in the field of education, there are several notable differences between South Korea on the one hand and Canada and the United States on the other.

2   First, the number of hours of study and formal training that Korean students go through in order to enter a university is much greater than that of either Canadians or Americans. People say that it is easy to graduate from a Korean university, but the really hard part is getting into the university in the first place. Because it's so difficult to get into a university in South Korea, most students not only attend their regular classes but also attend special "cram" schools for a few hours in the morning or afternoon. As a result, high school students in South Korea have fifty-five to sixty hours of instruction each week. This is in stark contrast to the situation in Canada and the United States, where secondary school students attend school less than thirty-five hours a week. In these North American countries, the most difficult years begin at age eighteen and don't let up until age twenty-two.

3   A second difference lies in society's attitude toward university education. In South Korea, competition to gain admittance to a prestigious university is intense. This competition results in an incredible amount of studying, dedication, and self-sacrifice as students do almost nothing but study for examinations. Parents feel this pressure as well and start training their children at a very young age for the eventual university exams. Thus, students feel pressure from their parents, their peers, and society in general. North American students may feel a comparable amount of pressure if they want to enter a school such as Harvard or Yale, but the average Canadian or American student does not have to deal with the societal pressure common in South Korea.

4   Finally, opportunities for university scholarships are very different in these countries. In Canada and the United States, there are academic scholarships, athletic scholarships, and scholarships for minority students. This allows for all types of students to take advantage of higher education at little or no cost. In South Korea, however, the most prevalent type of scholarship is the academic type. Sports skills, ethnic background, and other non-academic matters do not play a role in the awarding of university scholarships.

5   When people talk about educational differences between South Korea and Canada and the United States, they often focus on obvious differences such as school uniforms or extracurricular activities. However, these superficial differences are not nearly as important as the differences in the hours of study, society's attitude toward education, and scholarships. Despite these differences, the educational systems in all three countries continue to produce thousands of successful college graduates each year.

2.   In pairs or small groups, share the three hooks that you wrote with your classmates. Are any of them similar? Explain why you think your hooks will attract readers' attention.

| **Activity 9** | **Thesis Statement Questions** |

Answer these questions about the thesis statement in "Differences in Education in South Korea and North America."

1. What is the thesis statement in the essay?

   _____

   _____

2. Is this a direct or indirect thesis statement?

   Give the reason for your answer. _____

   _____

3. Rewrite the thesis statement as a direct thesis statement.

   _____

   _____

WRITING THE BODY

The body of an essay is the main part. It usually consists of three or four paragraphs between the introduction and the conclusion. The body follows a plan of organization that the writer usually determines before he or she starts writing. This organization varies depending on the kind of essay you are writing.

You can write the organizational plan of your essay in an outline. There are different levels of outlining. A **general outline** includes the main points, while a **specific,** or **detailed, outline** includes notes on even the smallest pieces of information. It is much easier to write an essay from a specific outline than from a general outline. However, most writers start with a general outline first and then add details.

WRITER'S NOTE: Using an Outline

The best essays have well-planned outlines that are carefully prepared before the writer starts writing.

Here is a **general outline** and a **specific outline** for Essay 7, "Differences in Education in South Korea and North America," pages 29–30. Read and compare the two outlines.

General Outline	Specific Outline
I. Introduction	I. Introduction
A. Hook: pose a question	A. Hook: Is education in South Korea really different from education in Canada or the U.S.?
B. Connecting information	B. Connecting information: We often hear of educational differences between South Korea and Canada/U.S., but the school systems are not so different on the surface. 1. Children start school at the same age. 2. Students attend school the same number of years.
C. Thesis: Differences in education between South Korea and the U.S./Canada	C. Thesis: There are several differences in education between South Korea and the U.S./Canada.
II. Body	II. Body
A. Difference #1: number of hours	A. Difference #1: number of hours 1. Hard to enter a Korean university but easy to graduate/exit 2. Korean students attend cram schools 3. Canada/U.S.=35 hrs/wk; Korea=55–60 hrs/wk

B. Difference #2: societal attitude toward education	B. Difference #2: societal attitude toward education
	1. Competition to enter a prestigious university
	  a. studying
	  b. dedication
	  c. self-sacrifice
	2. Pressure
	  a. from parents
	  b. from peers
	  c. from society in general
	3. North Americans don't have this pressure (except the few who enter Harvard/Yale).

C. Difference #3: scholarship opportunities

C. Difference #3: scholarship opportunities
   1. Canada/U.S.
      a. academic scholarships
      b. sports scholarships
      c. scholarships for minorities
   2. Korea
      a. only academic scholarships
      b. no role for sports/ethnicity

III. Conclusion
     (restate thesis statement)

III. Conclusion: Despite superficial differences, all three systems produce good graduates.

PRACTICE WITH OUTLINING AN ESSAY

General Outline

Activity 10   **Making a General Outline**

Here is a general outline for Essay 2, "How Do You Say . . . ?," (page 10). Read the essay again and complete this outline.

Title: _____

  I. Introduction (paragraph 1)

    A. Hook: Ask a general question

    B. Connecting information

    C. Thesis statement: _____

_____

  II. Body

    A. Paragraph 2 topic sentence: _____

_____

B. Paragraph 3 topic sentence: _____

_____

C. Paragraph 4 topic sentence: _____

_____

D. Paragraph 5 topic sentence: _____

_____

E. Paragraph 6 topic sentence: At first I was puzzled, but suddenly it all made sense.

III. Conclusion (paragraph 7)

A. End of action

B. Restatement of thesis

Specific Outline

| Activity 11 | Making a Specific Outline |

Here is a specific outline for Essay 1, "Cinderella and Her Odious Household Chores" on page 6. Read the essay again and complete this outline. You may use complete sentences if you wish, but be sure to include all of the specific information.

Title: "Cinderella and Her Odious Household Chores" _____

I. Introduction (paragraph 1)

A. Hook: _____

_____

B. Connecting information: _____

_____

_____

C. Thesis statement: _____

_____

II. Body

A. Paragraph 2

1. Topic sentence (chore #1): _____

_____

2. Supporting ideas

a. Attention to detail

(1) Smoothing out the fabric

(2) Following the seams

(3) _____

(4) _____

b. Problem: _____

_____

B. Paragraph 3

1. Topic sentence: (chore #2) _____

_____

2. Supporting ideas

a. Why we can't depend on dishwashers

b. Negative aspects of this chore

(1) Elbow grease

(2) _____

(3) _____

C. Paragraph 4

    1. Topic sentence (chore #3): _____

        _____

    2. Supporting ideas

        a. Tasks

            (1) _____

            (2) Cleaning the sink

            (3) Cleaning the toilet

        b. Negative aspects

            (1) Bathroom is full of germs

            (2) _____

        c. Positive aspect: _____

III. Conclusion (paragraph 5)

    A. Maintaining a house includes chores.

    B. Take pride in doing a good job and getting through the three odious chores.

WRITER'S NOTE: Outline Length

    If your outline is too long, combine some of the ideas or eliminate ideas that don't add interest to the essay.

WRITING THE CONCLUSION

    Some people think that writing the conclusion is the hardest part of writing an essay. For others, writing the conclusion is easy. When you write a conclusion, follow these guidelines:

1. Let the reader know that this is the conclusion. You can mark the conclusion with some kind of transition or connector that tells the reader that this is the final paragraph of the essay. (See Appendix 3 for a list of connectors.) Here are some examples:

   In conclusion,   From the information given,   To summarize,

   Sometimes the first sentence of the conclusion restates the thesis or main idea of the essay.

   This essay has presented three of the numerous problems that new parents face today.

2. Do not introduce new information in the conclusion. The conclusion should help the reader to reconsider the main ideas that you have given in the essay. Any new information in the concluding paragraph will sound like a continuation of the body of the essay.

3. Many writers find the conclusion difficult to write. It requires a great deal of thought and creativity, just as writing a good hook or thesis statement does. The kind of essay you are writing may determine the way you end the essay; however, two ideas can be helpful for any essay.

   a. The final sentence or sentences of an essay often give a *suggestion*, an *opinion*, or a *prediction* about the topic of the essay.

      • Suggestion:

         The facts strongly support the existence of a greenhouse warming effect on our atmosphere. It is vital, therefore, that we heed the warnings and do our best to keep this problem from getting worse.

      • Opinion:

         Certainly there are advantages and disadvantages to both of the plans presented here. However, because the second plan has more mass appeal than the former one, it would be a much better choice for the citizens of our country.

      • Prediction:

         This essay has presented strong arguments in favor of government control of television. Without this control, there will continue to be a decline in the moral values of American society.

   b. Sometimes the final sentence or sentences simply say that the issue has been discussed in the essay with so many strong, persuasive facts that the answer to the issue is now clear.

      Once aware of this information, any reader would have to agree that animal testing is cruel and unethical and should be abolished.

      After careful consideration of all the facts, readers will surely agree that the use of corporal punishment in our schools should be prohibited immediately.

WRITER'S NOTE: Check the First and Last Paragraphs

After you write your essay, read the introductory paragraph and the concluding paragraph. These two paragraphs should contain much of the same information without sounding exactly the same.

TOPICS FOR WRITING

Activity 12   **Essay Writing Practice**

Write an essay on one of the following suggested topics. Depending on the topic that you choose, you may need to do some research. Before you write, be sure to refer to the seven steps in the writing process in Appendix 1.

1. Write an essay about an important event that changed your life, such as marriage, the birth of a child, moving to a foreign country, or the loss of someone close to you.

2. Describe a festival or celebration in your culture. Discuss the history of the event, its meaning, and how it is celebrated.

3. Many inventions of the nineteenth century have changed our lives, such as television and the microwave oven. Write an essay in which you discuss the effects of one invention on society.

4. Some people say that people are born with their intelligence and outside factors do not affect intelligence very much. They believe that nature (what we are born with) is more important than nurture (environment). Other people say that intelligence is mostly the result of the interaction between people and their environment. These people believe that nurture is more important than nature. Write an essay in which you defend one of these points of view.

5. Write about a movie that you saw on television or at the cinema. Summarize the story and tell what you liked and didn't like about it.

Unit 2

Narrative Essays

GOAL: To learn how to write a narrative essay

LANGUAGE FOCUS: Connectors and time relationship words

WHAT IS A NARRATIVE ESSAY?

A narrative essay tells a story. Telling stories has always been an important part of human history. An essay that tells a story is called a *narrative* essay. Another word for *story* is *narrative*. Even though the narrative essay has the same basic form as most other academic essays, it allows the writer to be more creative than academic essays usually do.

Several important elements make up a story.

Setting	The setting is the location where the action in a story happens.
Theme	The theme is the basic idea of the story. Very often the theme will deal with a topic that is common in life or human nature, such as greed, envy, love, independence, and so on.
Mood	The mood is the feeling or atmosphere that the writer creates for the story. It could be happy, hopeful, suspenseful, scary. Both the setting and descriptive vocabulary create the mood in a narrative.
Characters	The characters are the people in the story. They are affected by the mood, and they react to the events in which they are involved.
Plot	The plot is what happens in the story, that is, the sequence of events. The plot often includes a climax or turning point at which the characters or events change.

THE INTRODUCTION

The introduction is the paragraph that begins your story. This is where you describe the setting, introduce the characters, and prepare the reader for the action to come. Of course, the introduction should have a hook and a thesis.

The Narrative Hook

You learned in Unit 1 that the hook in an essay is the part of the introduction—usually the first sentence or two—that grabs readers' attention. Hooks are especially important in narrative essays because they help "set the stage" for the story. The hook makes readers start guessing about what will happen next. Let's look at the hook from the essay in Activity 1.

> I had never been more anxious in my life. I had just spent the last three endless hours trying to get to the airport so that I could travel home.

Does this hook make you want to know what happened to the narrator? The hook should make the reader ask *wh-* questions about the essay. You may have thought of questions like these when you read the preceding example sentences:

> *Who* is the narrator and why is he or she anxious?
> *Where* is the airport?
> *What* made the trip to the airport seem endless?
> *Why* is this person going home?

Activity 1   Identifying Hooks

Read the sentences. Which three of these sentences are NOT good hooks for narrative essays? Put an X next to these sentences. Be ready to explain why you think these sentences do not work well as hooks for narrative essays.

1. _____ The roar of racecar engines ripped through the blazing heat of the day.

2. _____ It was freezing on that sad December day.

3. _____ After my brother's accident, I sat alone in the hospital waiting room.

4. _____ My friend and I shouldn't have been walking home alone so late on that dark winter night.

5. _____ Whales are by far the largest marine mammals.

6. _____ She gave her friend a birthday gift.

7. _____ The gleaming snow lay over the treacherous mountain like a soft white blanket, making the terrain seem safe instead of deadly.

8. _____ The Russian dictionary that we use in our language class has 500 pages.

9. _____ Sandra never expected to hear the deadly sound of a rattlesnake in her kitchen garden.

10. _____ A shot rang out in the silence of the night.

The Thesis

Usually the thesis states the main idea of the essay and tells what the organization of the information will be. However, in a narrative essay, the thesis introduces the action that begins in the first paragraph of the essay. Look at these example thesis statements:

> Now, as I watched the bus driver set my luggage on the airport sidewalk, I realized that my frustration had only just begun.

> I wanted my mother to watch me race down the steep hill, so I called out her name and then nudged my bike forward.

> Because his pride wouldn't allow him to apologize, Ken now had to fight the bully, and he was pretty sure that he wouldn't win.

The example sentences do not tell the reader what happens. They only introduce the action that will follow. The paragraphs in the body will develop the story.

THE BODY

The body of your narrative essay contains most of the plot—the supporting information. The action in the plot can be organized in many different ways. One way is **chronological,** or time, order. In this method each paragraph gives more information about the story as it proceeds in time: the first paragraph usually describes the first event, the second paragraph describes the second event, and so on.

Transitional Sentences

In a chronological organization, each paragraph ends with a **transitional sentence.** Transitional sentences have two purposes: (1) to signal the end of action in one paragraph, and (2) to provide a link to the action of the next paragraph. These sentences are vital because they give your story unity and allow the reader to follow the action easily. The following example is from Essay 8 on page 44, paragraphs 2 and 3. Notice how the ideas in the last sentence of paragraph 2 (the transitional sentence, underlined) and the first sentence of paragraph 3 (italicized) are connected.

EXAMPLE ESSAY

2 This was my first visit to the international section of the airport, and nothing was familiar. I couldn't make sense of the signs. Where was the ticket counter? Where should I take my luggage? I had no idea where the customs line was. I began to panic. What time was it? Where was my airplane? <u>I had to find help because I couldn't be late</u>!

3 *I tried to ask a passing businessman for help, but all my words came out wrong.* He just scowled and walked away. What had happened? I had been in this country for a whole semester, and I couldn't even remember how to ask for directions. This was awful! Another bus arrived at the terminal, and the passengers came out carrying all sorts of luggage. Here was my chance! I could follow them to the right place and I wouldn't have to say a word to them.

WRITER'S NOTE: Storytelling Tip

If you describe the sights, smells, and sounds of the story, you will bring the story alive for the reader.

THE CONCLUSION

Like academic essays, narrative essays need to have concluding ideas. In the **concluding paragraph,** you finish describing the action in the essay. The final sentence can have two functions:

1. It can deliver the moral for the story, or tell the reader what the character(s) learned from the experience.

2. It can make a prediction or a revelation (disclosure of something that was not known before) about future actions that will happen as a result of the events in the story.

Look at these examples:

Moral: The little boy had finally learned that telling the truth was the most important thing to do.

Prediction/   I can only hope that one day I will be able to do the same for
Revelation: another traveler who is suffering through a terrible journey.

                Every Christmas Eve, my wife and I return to that magical spot and remember the selfless act that saved our lives.

WRITER'S NOTE: Effective Narrative Essays

These are a few of the elements in an effective narrative essay:

- a thesis that sets up the action in the introduction
- transition sentences that connect events and help the reader follow the story
- a conclusion that ends the story action and provides a moral or revelation

EXAMPLE NARRATIVE ESSAY

A good way to learn what a narrative looks like is to read and study an example.

Activity 2   **Studying an Example Essay**

Read and study this narrative essay. Answer the questions. These questions will help you understand the content and the organization of the essay. As you read, look at the final sentence in paragraphs 2, 3, 4, and 5. Does each one prepare you for the action to come?

Essay 8

In this narrative essay, a traveler has a frustrating experience at the airport.
1. Have you ever had trouble trying to get to someplace very important? Where were you going? Why were you having problems?

2. What is a hero? What do you consider to be a heroic act?

Frustration at the Airport

1   I had never been more anxious in my life. I had just spent the last three endless hours trying to get to the airport so that I could travel home. Now, as I watched the bus driver set my luggage on the airport sidewalk, I realized that my frustration had only just begun.

2   This was my first visit to the international section of the airport, and nothing was familiar. I couldn't make sense of all the signs. Where was the ticket counter? Where should I take my luggage? I had no idea where the customs line was. I began to panic. What time was it? Where was my airplane? I had to find help because I couldn't be late!

3   I tried to ask a passing businessman for help, but all my words came out wrong. He just scowled and walked away. What had happened? I had been in this country for a whole semester, and I couldn't even remember how to ask for directions. This was awful! Another bus arrived at the terminal, and the passengers came out carrying all sorts of luggage. Here was my chance! I could follow them to the right place and I wouldn't have to say a word to them.

4   I dragged my enormous suitcase behind me and followed the group. We finally got to the elevators. Oh, no!! They all fit in, but there wasn't enough room for me. I watched in <u>despair</u> as the elevator doors closed. I had no idea what to do next. I got on the elevator when it returned and <u>gazed</u> at all the buttons. Which one would it be? I pressed button 3. The elevator slowly climbed up to the third floor and <u>jerked</u> to a stop. A high squeaking noise announced the opening of the doors, and I looked around <u>timidly</u>.

5   Tears formed in my eyes as I saw the deserted lobby and realized that I would miss my airplane. Just then an old airport employee <u>shuffled</u> around the corner. He saw that I was lost and asked if he could help. He gave me his handkerchief to dry my eyes as I related my <u>predicament</u>. He smiled kindly, took me by the hand, and led me down a long hallway. We walked up some stairs, turned a corner, and at last, there was customs! He led me past all the lines of people and pushed my luggage to the inspection counter.

6   When I turned to thank him for all his help, he was gone. I will never know that wonderful man's name, but I will always remember his unexpected <u>courtesy</u>. He helped me when I needed it the most. I can only hope that one day I will be able to do the same for another traveler who is suffering through a terrible journey.

frustration: feeling of impatience and discouragement

scowl: to frown

terminal: an arrival and departure point for some forms of mass transportation

despair: the condition of having no hope

gaze: to look at slowly and steadily

jerk: to move with an abrupt motion

timidly: hesitantly or fearfully

shuffle: to walk by sliding one's feet along the ground

predicament: a troubling situation

courtesy: a kind or polite action

WRITER'S NOTE: Verb Tense in Narrative Essays

Most narrative essays are written in the simple past tense because narratives usually tell events that have already happened.

3. What is the narrative hook?

    _____

    _____

4. Do you think the hook is effective (did it grab your attention)? Why, or why not?

    _____

    _____

5. Where is the setting of this story (where does it take place)?

    _____

6. What is the theme, or the basic idea, of "Frustration at the Airport"?

    _____

    _____

7. What do you think the mood of the story is? What feeling or atmosphere does the writer create?

    _____

    _____

8. Who are the characters?

    _____

    _____

9. What verb tense is used in "Frustration at the Airport"? _____ Write any five verbs here.

_____

_____

10. Is the story arranged in chronological, or time, order? In a few words, describe what happens first, second, third, and so on.

_____

_____

_____

_____

11. Underline the transitional sentences.

12. Does the story end with a moral or a revelation? If so, write it here:

_____

_____

Activity 3	**Outlining Practice**

Below is an outline for "Frustration at the Airport." Some of the information is missing. Reread the essay beginning on page 44 and complete the outline.

Title: _____

I. Introduction (paragraph 1)

    A. Hook: <u>I had never been so anxious in my life!</u> _____

    B. Connecting information _____

    C. Thesis statement: _____

    _____

II. Body

    A. Paragraph 2 (event 1) topic sentence:

    <u>This was my first visit to the international section of the airport, and nothing was familiar.</u>

SUPPORT

       1. The signs were confusing.

       2. I began to panic.

       3. Transition sentence:

       _____

    B. Paragraph 3 (event 2) topic sentence:

      _____

SUPPORT

       1. He scowled and walked away.

       2. I couldn't remember how to ask for directions.

       3. _____

       4. Transition sentence:

       _____

    C. Paragraph 4 (event 3) topic sentence:

    <u>I dragged my enormous suitcase behind me and followed the group.</u>

SUPPORT

       1. _____

       2. I got on the elevator and looked at the buttons.

       3. _____

       4. Transition sentence:

       _____

D. Paragraph 5 (event 4) topic sentence:

Tears formed in my eyes as I saw the deserted lobby and realized that I would miss my airplane

   1. An airport employee offered to help.

   2. _____

   3. _____

   3. Transition sentence: He led me past all the lines of people and pushed my luggage to

the inspection counter. _____

III. Conclusion (paragraph 6)

A. Close of the action:

_____

B. I will never know his name, but I will always remember his unexpected courtesy. _____

C. _____

D. Final sentence (prediction or revelation):

_____

Activity 4	**Adding Supporting Information**

The following narrative essay is missing large parts of the story (supporting information in the body). As you read, add information that moves the story along. Be sure to write transition sentences at the end of paragraphs 2, 3, and 4. If you need more space, use a separate piece of paper. Be as creative as you like!

Essay 9

You Make Your Own Luck

1   I should never have thrown the chain letter away. The letter warned me that if I did, I would have one day of bad luck. I didn't believe it, so I threw the silly thing in the garbage. I thought the friend who sent me the letter was just a superstitious fool. Letters don't bring you luck. You make your own! That night, however, as I feel asleep, I had the uncomfortable feeling that something was not quite right.

2   When I woke up the next morning, I was surprised to find that I had overslept and would be late for work. As I rushed down the stairs to eat a quick breakfast, I tripped over my cat and

_____

_____

_____

_____

3   On my way to work, I decided to take a shortcut through an old part of town. _____

_____

_____

_____

4   When I arrived at work, I found a note on my desk from my boss. She wanted to see me right away. I took a deep breath and walked into her office. As I stepped inside, I noticed a scowl on her face.

_____

_____

_____

_____

EXAMPLE ESSAY

5   Finally, after a long and difficult day, I returned home to find that my air conditioner was broken. I couldn't take it anymore! It had been the worst day of my life, and I didn't want anything else to happen. I rushed to the garbage can and dug around for the chain letter I had thrown away the day before. It was covered with coffee grounds and potato peels, but I could still read the words: "Send ten copies of this letter to your friends and you will have good luck for a year." I sat down at the kitchen table and began to make copies for ten of my friends. They could take their chances, but I wasn't going to have any more bad luck!

LANGUAGE FOCUS: Connectors and Time Relationship Words

The most common way to organize time in a narrative essay is in chronological order. The action that occurs first is in the introduction, and the actions that follow are in the next paragraphs (the body) and continue to the end (the conclusion).

To make sure that readers understand time relationships, effective writers of narrative essays use *connecting* words and phrases to show how events progress. Look at the lists of time words below. They contain some connectors that you can use in narrative writing. Brainstorm with your classmates to add more words to each list. (For a more complete list of connectors, see Appendix 3.)

Chronological Order	Prepositions	Time Words That Begin Clauses*
first (second, third, etc.)	after (a moment)	after
next	at (9:00 A.M.)	as soon as
finally	by (bedtime, then)	before
later	during (the afternoon)	(four weeks) later
now	until (five o'clock)	from then on
then		when
		while
		whenever
		until

*When time clauses occur at the beginning of a sentence, they MUST be followed by a comma.

Activity 5　　**Adding Connectors**

Read the next essay. Fill in the blanks with an appropriate connector, or time relationship word or phrase. Refer to the list in Language Focus.

Essay 10

The narrator tells about his friend's accident and what he (the narrator) learned from it.

A Little Bit of Rest Never Hurt Anyone

EXAMPLE ESSAY

1　　I have always been an active person. I love to swim and plays sports. I used to take

risks when I was having fun outdoors—until my good friend Carl had a little accident.

_____ I am a lot more careful about what I do.

EXAMPLE ESSAY

2   Carl has always been a biking enthusiast. He loves to ride his bright red mountain bike

in the hills outside of our town to get his daily workout. One day during a rainstorm, he

went out into the hills to ride his bike. The trails are very muddy and dangerous when it

rains, but he didn't let that stop him. _____ he was riding down the steepest

hill on the trail, he lost control of his bike. The bike skidded in the mud and he was flipped

over the handlebars. _____ he hit the ground, he landed on a large rock. He

was hurt pretty badly, and he had to be rushed to the emergency room in an ambulance.

3   _____ he got there, the nurses quickly cleaned his cuts and scratches.

_____ , they took him to get x-rays of both his legs and his shoulder. After

that, Carl saw the doctor, who said that he was lucky. Even though he was bruised all

over, only his shoulder was broken. _____ the doctor put a big, clumsy-

looking cast on Carl's shoulder. He told Carl that he would have to rest for the next six

weeks so that his body could heal properly.

EXAMPLE ESSAY

4 Because Carl was usually so active, he couldn't stay still. One week _____ the accident, he decided that he had to take a walk. As he was walking along, he tripped on the uneven sidewalk and lost his balance. He fell forward and landed on his new cast, and he broke it in half! As a result, he hurt his shoulder even more badly. He had to have a new cast put on. While he was there, the doctor scolded him and told him he that couldn't do anything at all _____ his bones had healed completely!

5 Even though I like adventure almost as much as Carl does, I have to admit that I learned many things from his misfortune. _____ , no matter how much you love to do something, you should always put safety first. _____ , if you are hurt, you should do what the doctors tell you or you might not recover well. _____ , a little bit of rest and quiet time never hurt anyone!

SENTENCE VARIETY WITH TIME WORDS

Essays that are written using only one or two sentence patterns can be dull to read. Good writers try to include variety in their sentences. Here are two ways to add variety with time words.

1. Follow the time word *after* with a noun.

change	Marta studied engineering at the University of Charleston. She graduated in 1996. Then she got a job with Johnson and Rowe, a local engineering firm.
to	Marta studied engineering at the University of Charleston. **After her graduation** in 1996, she got a job with Johnson and Rowe, a local engineering firm.

2. Follow *after, before, while,* and *when* with a gerund*.

change	A rare golden Sitka spruce was cut down by unknown vandals. It had been growing for more than three hundred years.
to	**After growing** for more than three hundred years, a rare golden Sitka spruce was cut down by unknown vandals.
change	Joanna Cannon ran for mayor. She promised to lower property taxes.
to	**While running** for mayor, Joanna Cannon promised to lower property taxes.

---

*A gerund is a verb form that ends in *-ing* and is used as a noun (*walking, studying*)

Activity 6   Sentence Variety

Read the following narrative essay. Then combine the sentences listed above the blanks into one sentence. Use the sentences in "Sentence Variety with Time Words" above as examples. Rewrite the sentences on the lines provided. You will not use all the words in the sentences when you combine them.

Essay 11

In this essay, the narrator tells about a frightening childhood accident.

The Reckless Rider

EXAMPLE ESSAY

1   On the day of my reckless adventure, my mother had finally stopped trying to make me behave. I could do whatever I wanted! Now I was free to explore the world! I rode my tricycle to the edge of the huge hill in our back yard and stopped.

• The hill was steep and scary. I looked down at it.

a. _When I looked down at it, the hill was steep and scary._

_____

I was thrilled by my adventure, so I tried it again. This time, I peddled my tricycle toward the hill much faster. It was so exciting!

• I built up some speed on my trip toward the edge. I suddenly got scared.

b. _____

_____

I wanted to stop, but I couldn't. I shrieked as I hurtled over the edge and down the hill. 2   The next thing I knew, I was at the bottom of the hill. My head hurt terribly. Even worse, all the air was knocked out of me when I hit the ground. I panicked as I desperately tried to draw air into my lungs. My mouth was open, but I couldn't get any air.

• My mother rushed over to me. She put her hands on my shoulders. She began talking to me.

c. _____

_____

She urged me to take deep breaths and told me that everything would be fine. I wasn't sure that she was right.

3 Finally, my windpipe opened and I sucked in some air. When I had enough oxygen to breathe normally again, I began to cry. My tears were caused not only by the pain in my head but also by fear. My mother picked me up and held me tightly. I think she was as frightened by the fall as I was. She took me to the kitchen and put ice on the bump that had formed on my head.

• She gave me a cookie. At the same time, she scolded me for being so reckless.

d. _____

She also told me never to go near the hill without an adult. She didn't need to worry about that! I never went near there alone again. To this day, I still feel nervous when I see a steep hill.

DEVELOPING NARRATIVE ESSAYS

There are a few strategies in particular that can help you write and edit your narrative essay, such as choosing a topic, brainstorming, and making an outline.

CHOOSING A TOPIC

When you write a narrative essay, it is important to keep in mind that smaller is better. The smaller the action or event you choose, the easier it will be to keep your readers' interest and describe the action fully. For example, it would be impossible to describe—in one essay—all the events that helped make you the person you are today. However, you could choose one event that made a difference in your life, such as your first job or a special award, and write an essay about that. At the same time, be careful that the topic you choose is not too small. For example, a story about how your little brother called you a name one day would not be a good topic for a narrative essay. There should be enough action to make a story of five or six paragraphs.

WRITER'S NOTE: Topic Tip

When you think about topics, try to remember something exciting, difficult, wonderful, or frightening that has happened to you. Can this event be developed into an interesting narrative essay?

Ask Yourself Questions

To help think of some possible topics for narrative essays, ask yourself questions. Use these as a guide:

- When was an important time in my life?

- What has happened in my experience that I would enjoy writing about?

- Is there an event in my life that other people (readers) would enjoy hearing about?

- How did I feel about a particular experience?

- Who was involved?

- Why do I remember this event so strongly? What effect did it have on me?

- Did anything change because of this experience?

- What interesting experiences do I know of that happened to other people?

If you are answering some of these questions about a specific experience that you or someone else had, then you may have a topic for a narrative essay.

Activity 7	Choosing Topics

Look at the pairs of topics. Put an X next to the topic that is the better choice for a narrative essay.

1. _____ Your last year in high school

   _____ Your last day in high school

2. _____ A scary airplane ride to another city

   _____ A scary trip around the world

3. _____ Buying a washing machine

   _____ Buying your first car

4. _____ Important religious ceremonies that you have participated in

   _____ Your brother's embarrassing wedding ceremony

5. _____ What I did last New Year's Eve

   _____ What I did last year

Activity 8	**Ideas for a Narrative Essay**

Take a few minutes to think about possible topics for a narrative essay. Write some ideas here.

_____

_____

_____

IDEAS BRAINSTORMING

   Brainstorming is a process by which you generate ideas about essay topics. There are many ways to brainstorm for a narrative essay. Here you will take a brief look at three different ways to develop ideas for your narrative essay.

   1. Ask *wh-* questions about your topic. With this method, you begin with a general idea of the topic that you're interested in. Then ask the questions *who? what? when? where? why?* and in some cases *how?* The answers to these questions will help clarify what you would like to write about. Here's an example:

   General topic: Celebrating Independence Day

   Questions: *Who* celebrates Independence Day?
            What is the history of this celebration?
            When does the celebration take place?
            Where do people celebrate?
            Why do they celebrate?
            How do they celebrate Independence Day?

   2. Make a list of words or phrases that describe your topic. This list can help

with vocabulary choices when you write your essay. Here is a sample list on the topic of "U.S. Independence Day":

patriotism	red, white, and blue	warm weather
fireworks	freedom	parades
picnic	sports	veterans
loud noises	family	flag

3. Make a visual map of your essay ideas. One kind of visual map is called *clustering*. To cluster, write your topic in the center of a sheet of paper and then circle it. On lines that come out from the circle, begin writing words and ideas associated with the topic. Write whatever comes to mind. Connect any words that are related. When you are finished, you will have many new ideas about your topic.

Here is an example of clustering on the topic of American Independence Day.

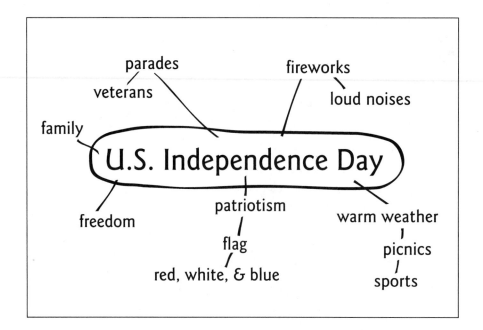

WRITER'S NOTE: Brainstorming Tips

Remember these important points about brainstorming:

- Use just one of these brainstorming techniques or a combination of them.
- Choose a subject that you can write about in approximately five or six paragraphs.
- Choose a topic that is important to you—your essay will be easier to write and more interesting to read if you do.
- When you brainstorm, don't worry about correct grammar or spelling.

Activity 9   **Developing Narrative Ideas**

1. Choose a topic that is suitable for a narrative essay. You may want to look at your notes from Activity 8 to help you. Remember that in a narrative essay, you tell a story. Work with other students to see if your topic is appropriate.

2. After you have a suitable topic, brainstorm some ideas about your topic. You may use any brainstorming method that you prefer. Use separate paper.

3. Now it's time to begin organizing your ideas. Remember that it's not necessary to tell every detail of the story. Include only the most important actions or events that move the story forward. Write some ideas here.

   a. Introduction (beginning of the story): theme, setting, and characters

      What is the basic idea of the story? Where is the story taking place? When is the story taking place? Who is in the story?

      _____

      _____

      _____

   b. Body (middle of the story): mood and plot

      What feeling or atmosphere do you want to create in your story? What will happen in the plot?

      _____

      _____

      _____

      _____

   c. Conclusion (end of the story): finish of the action, moral or prediction/revelation

      What will happen last in your story? How will you finish the plot? Will your narrative essay have a moral or make a prediction or a revelation?

      _____

      _____

      _____

Activity 10   **Making an Outline**

Use the outline below as a guide to help you make a more detailed plan for your narrative essay. You may need to use either more or fewer points under each heading. Include your ideas from Activity 8. Where possible, write in complete sentences.

TOPIC: _____

     I. Introduction (paragraph 1)

        A. Hook: _____

           _____

        B. Connecting information: _____

           _____

        C. Thesis statement: _____

           _____

    II. Body

        A. Paragraph 2 (event 1) topic sentence: _____

           _____

SUPPORT

           1. _____

           2. _____

           3. Transition sentence: _____

           _____

        B. Paragraph 3 (event 2) topic sentence: _____

           _____

SUPPORT

1. _____

2. _____

3. Transition sentence: _____

_____

C. Paragraph 4 (event 3) topic sentence: _____

_____

SUPPORT

1. _____

2. _____

3. Transition sentence: _____

_____

D. Paragraph 5 (event 4) topic sentence: _____

_____

SUPPORT

1. _____

2. _____

3. Transition sentence: _____

_____

III. Conclusion (paragraph 6)

A. Close of the action: _____

_____

B. _____

_____

C. _____

D. Final sentence (prediction or revelation): _____

_____

ABOUT PEER EDITING

Many students think that writing a paper once is enough. This is rarely true. Even skilled and professional writers write and edit more than one draft.

Think of the first draft of your essay as your first attempt. Before you rewrite, it's helpful to let someone read your paper, offer comments, and ask questions about your meaning. Many writers don't always see their own mistakes, but a reader can help you see where you need to make improvements.

Sometimes you need more than one opinion about your essay. In class, peer editing is an easy way to get opinions. With this method, other students (your peers) read your essay and make comments using a set of questions and guidelines (in Appendix 4). You will read someone else's essay, too. Peer editing can help you clear up any areas that are not strong or that seem confusing to the reader.

WRITER'S NOTE: Suggestions for Peer Editing

- *Listen carefully.* In peer editing, you will receive many comments and some suggestions from other students. It is important to listen carefully to comments about your writing. You may think that what you wrote is clear and accurate, but readers can often point out places that need improvement. Remember that the comments are about the writing, not about you!

- *Make helpful comments.* When you read your classmates' essays, choose your words and comments carefully so that you don't hurt their feelings. For example, instead of saying, "This is bad grammar" or "I can't understand any of your ideas," make helpful comments, such as, "You need to make sure that every sentence has a verb" or "What do you mean in this sentence?"

Activity 11	Peer Editing Your Outline

Exchange outlines with another student. Read each other's outlines and make comments using Peer Editing Sheet 1 on page 151.

Activity 12 ▪ Writing a Narrative Essay

Write a narrative essay based on the outline that you completed in Activity 9. Save all your work, including your brainstorming pages or notes, revised drafts, and Peer Editing Sheet 1. Be sure to refer to the seven steps in the writing process in Appendix 1 on page 126.

Activity 13 ▪ Peer Editing Your Essay

Exchange narrative essays from Activity 12 with a partner. Then use Peer Editing Sheet 2 on page 153 to help you comment on your partner's paper. It is important to offer positive comments that will help the writer.

TOPICS FOR WRITING

Activity 14 ▪ Essay Writing Practice

Here are more ideas for topics for a narrative essay. Before you write, be sure to refer to the seven steps in the writing process in Appendix 1.

1. Write a story that tells why a certain place is special to you. What does this place mean to you? What happened there?

2. Think of a person that you know well. Be sure that you feel comfortable writing about him or her. Tell a story about this person. How did he or she influence you? What unusual or exciting experience has this person had?

3. Write about an important event in history from the point of view of someone who lived at that time.

4. Choose a piece of music and listen to it. When you hear the music, what do you imagine is happening? Create a story that describes what is happening in the music.

5. Tell a story about an important event that happened in your family's history. Tell it from the point of view of one of the main characters.

Unit 3

Comparison Essays

GOAL: To learn how to write a comparison essay

LANGUAGE FOCUS: Connectors for comparison essays

You make comparisons between things all the time, for example, whenever you have to make a decision. What will you eat for breakfast, cereal or a bagel? Where will you live, in an apartment or a dormitory? What will you study at the university, physics or mathematics? In order to make your decision, you look at the merits of each choice. You compare their differences and similarities. Then you choose the best option.

WHAT IS A COMPARISON ESSAY?

In a comparison essay, you compare things. The subjects of this kind of essay are two ideas that are related in some way. You can focus on the similarities between the two things, on the differences, or on both the similarities and the differences. Your goal is to show your readers how these subjects are similar or different, what their strengths and weaknesses are, or what their advantages and disadvantages are.

Like other essays, the comparison essay has an introductory paragraph that contains a hook and a thesis statement, three or four body paragraphs, and a concluding paragraph. (See Unit 1 for a review of the structure of an essay.)

PATTERNS OF ORGANIZATION

There are two basic ways to organize a comparison essay, the block method and the point-by-point method.

Block Method

With the block method, you present one subject and all its points of comparison before you do the same for the second subject. With this organization, you discuss each subject completely without interruption.

Here is an example of the organization of a comparison essay about the social behavior of Russians and Americans.

Introduction	paragraph 1	hook, thesis
Body	paragraphs 2–3	Russian social behavior
		• at parties
		• in school
		• at home
	paragraphs 4–5	American social behavior
		• at parties
		• in school
		• at home
Conclusion	paragraph 6	restated thesis, opinion

Point-by-Point Method

With the point-by-point method, you present both subjects under one point of comparison before moving on to the next point. Here is an example of the topic of the social behavior of Russians and Americans, organized with the point-by-point method.

Introduction	paragraph 1	hook, thesis
Body	paragraph 2	At parties • Russian social behavior • American social behavior
	paragraph 3	In school • Russian social behavior • American social behavior
	paragraph 4	At home • Russian social behavior • American social behavior
Conclusion	paragraph 5	restated thesis, opinion

With both the point-by-point and the block method, the writer sometimes ends with an opinion as to which of the two subjects is preferable.

WRITER'S NOTE: Parallel Organization of Supporting Information

In the block method example, notice that the supporting information in paragraphs 2 and 3 includes parties, school, and home. The supporting information in paragraphs 4 and 5 also includes these three topics. In the point-by-point method example, the supporting information includes parties, school, and home, but information about each society is presented under each idea before going on to the next.

These repeated structures are called *parallel organization*. No matter which overall method of organization you choose, parallel organization is required of your information in all comparison essays.

CHOOSING A METHOD OF ORGANIZATION

How do you know which method of organization is better for your comparison essay? Consider the following information about each method.

Block method:
• You develop each subject completely, without interruption.

- It may be difficult for readers to see the parallel points of comparison between your two subjects. Some rereading or more critical reading of certain parts of the essay may be necessary.

Point-by-point method:

- Both subjects are presented in each paragraph, so readers go back and forth between the two subjects.
- The parallel points of comparison may be easier to see.

As you decide which method to use, consider your subjects (how complex are they?), your readers (which method will make it easier for them to follow these particular subjects?), and your writing style (which method are you more comfortable with?).

EXAMPLE COMPARISON ESSAY

A good way to learn how to write a comparison essay is to study an example.

Activity 1   Studying an Example Essay

Read and study the following comparison essay. Work with a partner to answer the questions before and after the essay. These questions will help you understand the content and the organization of the essay.

Essay 12

In this essay, the writer compares some features of Brazil and the United States.

1. What do you know about the different cultural groups that live in Brazil and the United States?
2. What does the word *individualism* mean?

Not As Different As You Think

1 All countries in the world are unique. They are different from one another in location, size, culture, government, climate, and lifestyles. However, many countries share similarities. Some may think that because Brazil and the United States are in different <u>hemispheres</u>, these two

EXAMPLE ESSAY

·nations have nothing in common. On the contrary, they share many similarities.

2   One important similarity is their size. Both Brazil and the United States are large countries. Brazil covers almost half of the South American continent. Few Brazilians can say that they have traveled <u>extensively</u> within its borders. Because of Brazil's large size, its weather varies greatly from one area to another. Like Brazil, the United States takes up a significant portion of its continent (North America), so most Americans have visited only a few of the fifty states. In addition, the United States has a wide range of <u>climates</u>. While the Northeast is experiencing snowstorms, cities like Miami, Florida, can have temperatures over 85 degrees Fahrenheit.

3   Another similarity between Brazil and the United States is the diversity of ethnic groups. Brazil was colonized by Europeans, and its culture has been greatly influenced by this fact. However, the identity of the Brazilian people is not <u>solely</u> a product of Western civilization. Brazil is a "melting pot" of many ethnic groups that immigrated there and mixed with the native people. The United States also has a diversity of ethnic groups representing the early colonists from northern Europe as well as groups from Africa, the Mediterranean, Asia, and South America. The mixture of cultures and customs has worked to form ethnically rich cultures in both countries.

4   Finally, <u>individualism</u> is an important value for both Brazilians and Americans. Brazil works hard to defend the <u>concept</u> of freedom of choice. Citizens believe that they have the right to do and be whatever they desire as long as they don't hurt others. Individualism and freedom of choice also exist in the United States, where freedom is perhaps the highest value of the people. Some may believe that the desire for individual expression is divisive and can make a country weak. However, the ability of people to be whatever they want makes both countries strong.

5   Although Brazil and the United States are unique countries, there are remarkable similarities in their size, ethnic groups, and personal values. Some people tend to believe that their culture and country are without equal. Nevertheless, it is important to remember that people as a whole have more in common than they generally think they do.

hemisphere: one half of the world

extensively: widely; over a large area

climate: the usual weather of a region over a
  period of time

solely: only; entirely

individualism: the belief that each person works
  for his or her own goals

concept: idea

3. What subjects does the writer compare in this essay?

_____

4. What method of organization does the writer use, point-by-point or block?

_____

5. What is the hook for this essay? Write it here.

_____

6. Underline the thesis statement. Is the thesis restated in the conclusion (paragraph 5)? If yes,
   underline that sentence in the conclusion.

7. Supporting sentences: In paragraph 2, the author writes about the ways in which size affects Brazil
   and the United States. List that information here.

The Effects of Size

Brazil	United States
1. _____	1. _____
_____	_____
2. _____	2. _____
_____	_____
3. _____	3. _____
_____	_____

8. Reread the concluding paragraph of "Not As Different As You Think." Does the writer offer **a suggestion, an opinion,** or **a prediction**? Circle the appropriate phrase in bold and write the sentence from the essay.

_____

_____

DEVELOPING COMPARISON ESSAYS

In this next section, you will develop comparison essays as you make an outline, write supporting information, study connectors, and choose a topic. In the following activities, you will practice the skills you need to write an effective comparison essay.

Activity 2	Outlining Practice

Below is a specific outline for "Not As Different As You Think." (For a review of specific outlines, see pages 31–36.) Some of the information is missing. Reread the essay beginning on page 67 and complete the outline.

Title: _____

I. Introduction (paragraph 1)

   A. Hook: _All countries in the world are unique._____

   B. Connecting information: Different location, size, culture

   C. Thesis statement: _____

   _____

II. Body

   A. Paragraph 2 (similarity 1) topic sentence: _____

   _____

SUPPORT

1. Brazil's characteristics

   a. Size: _____

   b. Travel: Few Brazilians have traveled extensively in their country.

   c. Climate: _____

2. _____

   a. _____

   b. Travel: _____

   c. Climate: The weather can be extremely different from the north to the south.

B. Paragraph 3 (similarity 2) topic sentence:

Another similarity is the diversity of ethnic groups.

SUPPORT

1. Brazil

   a. _____

   b. Other ethnic groups.

   c. _____

2. U.S.

   a. Europe

   b. Africa

   c. the Mediterranean

   d. _____

   e. _____

C. Paragraph 4 (similarity 3) topic sentence:

_____

SUPPORT

   1. Brazilians' belief in freedom: _____

_____

   2. _____

_____

III. Conclusion (paragraph 5)

   A. Restated thesis: _____

_____

   B. Opinion: Nevertheless, it is important to remember that people as a whole have more in common than they generally think they do.

WRITER'S NOTE: Ask Questions

   How can you develop details and facts that will support your main ideas (topic sentences) in each paragraph? One of the best ways to write this supporting information is to ask yourself questions about the topic—*Where? Why? When? Who? What? How?*

Activity 3   **Supporting Information**

The following comparison essay is missing the supporting information. As you read the essay, work with a partner to write supporting sentences for each paragraph. If you need more space, use a separate piece of paper. After you finish, compare your supporting information with that of other students.
   Note: This essay follows the point-by-point organizational pattern.

Essay 13

   Many car buyers want to know the differences between foreign and domestic cars. In this essay, you and the writer provide some of that information.

Foreign or Domestic?

1 Transportation today is much different from the way it was fifty years ago. At that time, people who wanted to buy an automobile had a small variety to choose from. Nowadays, there are so many choices that it could take months to look at all the cars on the market. Often a buyer must first choose between a foreign car and a domestic car. To reach a decision, a buyer should compare foreign and domestic cars in terms of quality and dependability, maintenance, and style.

2 Foreign and domestic cars vary in quality and dependability. _____

_____

_____

_____

_____

_____

3 Another thing to consider is maintenance. _____

_____

_____

_____

_____

EXAMPLE ESSAY

4 Finally, there is the subject of style. _____

_____

_____

_____

_____

_____

5 All cars are used for transportation, but it is important to remember that there are differences in quality and dependability, service options, and style, depending on the make and model. Choosing a domestic vehicle or an imported one is a personal decision. Careful consideration of the information presented here will make choosing a car less complicated.

LANGUAGE FOCUS: Connectors for Comparison Essays

Writers use connectors in a well-organized essay to help clarify the main ideas. Connectors help readers by providing logical connections between sentences, ideas, and paragraphs. Notice that when these words (sometimes including the phrase that follows) begin sentences, they are followed by a comma.

The following two charts show connectors that can be used in comparison essays. Notice that the first chart is for comparison words and phrases and the second chart is for contrast words and phrases. (For a more complete list of connectors, see Appendix 3.)

Connectors That Show Comparison

Between sentences or paragraphs	Example
In addition,	Both Red Beauty and Midnight Dream roses are known for the size of their blooms, their color, and their fragrance. **In addition,** they are easy to grow.
Similarly,	The Midnight Dream rose won awards in local contests last year. **Similarly,** the Red Beauty Rose was singled out for its beauty.
Likewise,	The blooms of Red Beauty roses last longer than those of most other roses. **Likewise,** the blooms of the Midnight Dream rose are long-lasting.

Compared to . . . ,

Compared to many other roses, the blooms of Red Beauty and Midnight Dream roses last a long time.

Connectors That Show Contrast

Between sentences or paragraphs	Example
However, On the other hand,	**However, (On the other hand,)** some of their differences are not very obvious.
In contrast,	Red Beauty has a strong, sweet fragrance. **In contrast,** Midnight Dream's fragrance is light and fruity.
Although . . . ,	**Although** they both have red flowers, Midnight Dream roses are darker than Red Beauty roses.
Even though . . . ,	**Even though** they are both long-stemmed roses, Red Beauty stems are thin and covered with thorns while Midnight Dream stems are thick and have almost no thorns.
Unlike . . . ,	**Unlike** Red Beauty, Midnight Dream roses are relatively inexpensive.

Activity 4   Connectors

Read the next student essay and circle the appropriate connector in parentheses. Refer to the list in Language Focus, if necessary.

Essay 14

The writer in this essay compares the educational systems in Taiwan and the United States.

Education in the East and the West

EXAMPLE ESSAY

1   Americans have often asked me why I came from Taiwan to study in the United States. They expect me to say something like "to learn English." (*However/Another*), to me, coming here to study involves more than just learning English. It involves an opportunity to experience a completely different educational system. Because I have

studied in both countries, I have seen several areas in which education in Taiwan and education in the United States are different.

2   Students' expectations in the classroom in Taiwan are different from those in the United States. Generally speaking, Taiwanese students are quieter and participate less in class. They are not encouraged to express their ideas unless asked. They are taught that asking teachers a question is seen as a challenge to the teacher's authority. There is little emphasis on developing student creativity and thinking skills. Students are expected to memorize everything they are assigned. (*In addition/However*), in the United States the curriculum emphasizes individual thinking, group discussion, and self-expression. (*Unlike/Even though*) their Taiwanese counterparts, American students are encouraged to ask questions, express their own opinions, and think for themselves.

3   (*However/In addition*), there is a great disparity in the educational goals of Taiwanese and American schools. After twelve years of compulsory education, Taiwanese students have to pass an entrance exam in order to get into a university. The higher students score on this test, the better the university they can enter. Taiwanese culture puts a strong emphasis on

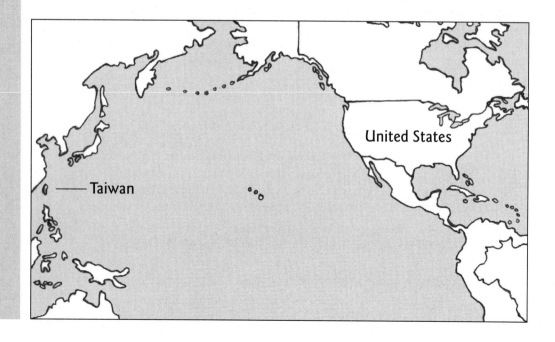

United States

Taiwan

university admission because getting into the right university can guarantee future success. As a result, schools often "teach to the test" instead of providing more moral, social, and physical education. (*In contrast/Likewise*), the goals of the American educational system include teaching students how to learn and helping them reach their maximum potential. American teachers give their students the freedom to think and solve problems on their own; they do not merely prepare students to answer questions for an entrance exam.

4   The last obvious difference between the two countries' educational systems is the role of extracurricular activities such as sports programs and special interest clubs. (*Even though/Compared to*) every Taiwanese school claims that it pays equal attention to moral, intellectual, and physical education, the real focus is on passing the university admissions exam. Little emphasis is placed on activities outside of the classroom. Teachers can even borrow time from extracurricular activities to give students more practice in the areas where they have weaknesses. (*On the other hand/Likewise*), American educational institutions consider the development of social and interpersonal skills as important as the development of intellectual skills. It is believed that by participating in these outside activities, students can demonstrate their special talents, level of maturity, and leadership qualities.

5   Education is vital to everyone's future success. While it may take ten years to grow a tree, a sound educational system may take twice as long to take root. (*However/Although*) Taiwan and the United States have different educational systems, both countries have the same ultimate goal: to educate their citizens as well as they can. This goal can be reached only if people take advantage of all the educational opportunities given to them. That is why I came to the United States to study, grow, and become a better person.

BRAINSTORMING

You will be asked to write comparison essays in many of your classes. Often, you will be given the two subjects to be compared, such as two works of literature, two kinds of chemical compounds, or two political beliefs. When you have to choose your own subjects for comparison, the following brainstorming tips will help you.

Tips for brainstorming subjects

1. The subjects should have something in common.

   Soccer and hockey are both fast-paced games that require a player to score a point by putting an object into a goal guarded by another player.

2. The two subjects must also have some differences.

   The most obvious differences between the two games are the playing field, the protective equipment, and the number of players.

3. You need to have enough information on each topic to make your comparisons.

   If you choose two sports that are not well-known, it might be more difficult to find information about them.

Make a list

A good way to determine whether you have enough information about similarities and differences between two subjects is to brainstorm a list. Read the information in the lists below.

Ice Hockey

played on ice

6 players on a team

uses a puck

(very popular sport)

(players use lots of protective pads)

(can't touch the puck with your hands)

(goal = puck in the net)

Soccer

played on a grass field

11 players on a team

uses a soccer ball

(very popular sport)

(players use some protective pads)

(can't touch the ball with your hands)

(goal = ball in the net)

As you can see, soccer and hockey have many similarities and a few differences. Notice that the similarities are circled. These are "links" between the two subjects. A writer could use these links to highlight the similarities between the two games or to lead into a discussion of the differences between them ("Although both soccer and hockey are popular, more schools have organized soccer teams than hockey . . . ").

Make a Venn diagram

Another way to brainstorm similarities and differences is to use a Venn diagram. (Perhaps you have used Venn diagrams in math class.) A Venn diagram is a visual representation of the similarities and differences between two concepts. Here is a Venn diagram of the characteristics of hockey and soccer.

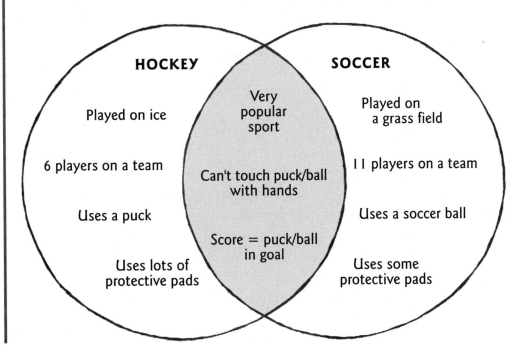

Activity 5   Identifying Good Subjects

Below are pairs of potential subjects for a comparison essay. Write "yes" on the line under the pairs that would be good subjects and explain briefly what could be compared. Write "no" next to the subjects that would not be good choices and change one or both of them into more suitable subjects. The first two have been done for you as examples.

1. living in houses / living in apartments

   Yes. Compare costs, privacy, space _____

2. international travel / 747 airplanes

   No. Change "747 airplanes" to "domestic travel" _____

3. high school / college

   _____

4. the weather in Toronto / tourist attractions in Toronto

   _____

5. wild animals / animals in a zoo

   _____

6. computers / computer keyboards

   _____

7. hands / feet

   _____

8. the surface of the ocean floor / the surface of the continents

   _____

9. the Earth / the North American continent

   _____

10. Chinese food / Mexican food

_____

WRITER'S NOTE: Writing from Personal Experience

Many international students like to compare and contrast certain features of their cultures to those of other cultures. These topics usually lead to interesting essays that engage readers.

Activity 6   **Working with a Topic**

1. Choose one topic from the list or use your own idea for a topic. If you want to use an original idea, talk to your teacher to see if it is appropriate for a comparison essay.

two famous people	two sports	two movies
two places	two machines	two celebrations or holidays
two kinds of behavior	two kinds of education	two kinds of storms

2. Use the following chart to brainstorm a list of information about each subject. If you like, use the soccer/hockey list on page 79 as a guide.

TOPIC: _____

Subject 1   Subject 2

_____   _____

_____   _____

_____   _____

_____   _____

_____   _____

_____   _____

_____   _____

3. Now fill in the Venn diagram using the information from the preceding chart.

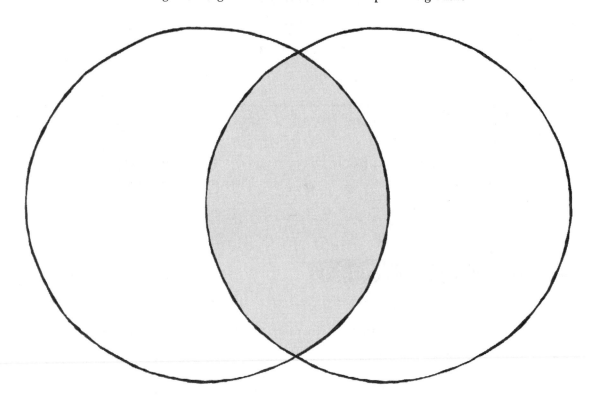

4. Decide if you are going to compare mainly the similarities or the differences or both between the two subjects in your comparison essay. Then choose three or four main points that you will use and list them here.

a. _____

b. _____

c. _____

d. _____

WRITER'S NOTE: Ideas for Supporting Information

In the next activity, you will develop supporting information. Here are some ideas to help you get started. For a point of comparison,

- give a description.
- give examples.
- give a cause.
- give an effect.

Activity 7	Planning with an Outline

Now that you have a topic, it's time to create an outline for your comparison essay. Use the outline below as a guide to help you brainstorm a more detailed plan for your essay. For this activity, use the point-by-point method of organization (see page 66). You may need to use either more or fewer points under each heading. Include your ideas from Activity 6. Write complete sentences where possible.

TOPIC: _____

    I. Introduction (paragraph 1)

        A. Hook: _____

        B. Connecting information: _____

        _____

        C. Thesis statement: _____

        _____

    II. Body

        A. Paragraph 2 (first point of comparison) topic sentence: _____

        _____

SUPPORT

            1. _____

                a. _____

                b. _____

            2. _____

                a. _____

                b. _____

B. Paragraph 3 (second point of comparison) topic sentence: _____

_____

SUPPORT

   1. _____

      a. _____

      b. _____

   2. _____

      a. _____

      b. _____

C. Paragraph 4 (third point of comparison) topic sentence: _____

_____

SUPPORT

   1. _____

      a. _____

      b. _____

   2. _____

      a. _____

      b. _____

III. Conclusion (paragraph 5)

  A. Restated thesis: _____

_____

  B. Suggestion, opinion, or prediction: _____

_____

Activity 8   **Peer Editing Your Outline**

Exchange outlines with another student. Read each other's outlines and make comments using Peer Editing Sheet 3 on page 155.

Activity 9   **Writing a Comparison Essay**

After you have read your classmate's review of your outline, think about any changes you want to make in your essay. Make sure you have enough information to develop your supporting sentences. Then write your comparison essay. Save all your work, including your brainstorming pages or notes, revised drafts, and the Peer Editing Sheet. Be sure to refer to the seven steps in the writing process in Appendix 1 on page 126.

Activity 10   **Peer Editing Your Essay**

Exchange comparison essays from Activity 9 with a partner. Then use Peer Editing Sheet 4 on page 157 to help you comment on your partner's paper. It is important to offer positive comments that will help the writer.

TOPICS FOR WRITING

Activity 11   **Essay Writing Practice**

Here are more ideas for topics for a comparison essay. Before you write, be sure to refer to the seven steps in the writing process in Appendix 1.

1. Compare a book to its movie version, for example, *The Great Gatsby* by F. Scott Fitzgerald. How are the two alike and different? Are the characters and the plot the same? Do you like the movie or the book better, and why?

2. Compare the situation in a country before and after an important historical event, for example, Cuba before and after Fidel Castro came to power.

3. Discuss two kinds of music, such as classical and rock. A few points of comparison might be artists, instruments, audiences, and popularity.

4. Show how the world has changed since the invention of the airplane. How did people travel before its invention? How often did people travel? How far were they usually able to go and how long did it take to get there?

5. Show the similarities and differences in the ways that two cultures celebrate an important event such as a birthday, wedding, or funeral.

Unit 4

Cause-Effect Essays

GOAL: To learn how to write a cause-effect essay

LANGUAGE FOCUS: Connectors for cause-effect essays

WHAT IS A CAUSE-EFFECT ESSAY?

A cause-effect essay shows the reader the relationship between something that happens and its consequences, or between actions and results. For example, if too much commercial fishing is allowed in the North Atlantic Ocean (action), the fish population in some areas may diminish or disappear (result). Cause-effect essays can be informative and insightful.

You will study two kinds of cause-effect essays. Very simply, in one method, the writer focuses on the *causes* of something. This is called the **Focus-on-Cause** method. In the second method, the writer emphasizes the effects or *results* of a cause. This is called the **Focus-on-Effect** method.

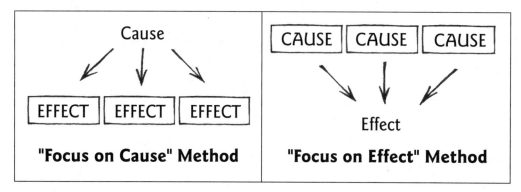

Imagine that your teacher gives you the topic of culture shock to write about. You have the choice of writing either a cause essay or an effect essay.

FOCUS-ON-CAUSE METHOD

If you decide to use the focus-on-cause method, you would focus mainly on the causes of culture shock—perhaps three or four things that lead people to suffer from culture shock. Each paragraph would address one of these ideas. You might begin with this question: **Why do people feel culture shock?**

FOCUS-ON-EFFECT METHOD

On the other hand, you may want to emphasize the effects of culture shock—perhaps three or four things that people with culture shock feel or experience. By choosing the focus-on-effect method, your body paragraphs would explain how culture shock affects people. Each paragraph would address one idea. You might begin with this question: **What happens to people who experience culture shock?**

WRITER'S NOTE: Cause-Effect Essay Methods

Essays that use the focus-on-cause method answer the question "Why does something happen?"

Essays that use the focus-on-effect method answer the question "What happens when . . . ?"

EXAMPLE CAUSE-EFFECT ESSAY

A good way to help you learn how to write a cause-effect essay is to study an example. The following example is a cause essay that answers the question "Why do people lie?"

Activity 1 | **Studying an Example Essay**

Read and study the following essay. Work with a partner to answer the questions before and after the essay. These questions will help you understand the content and the organization of the essay.

Essay 15

This essay may make you think twice before you tell another lie.

1. Why do you think people lie?

2. Is it ever acceptable to lie? Give examples of acceptable and unacceptable lies.

Why Do We Lie?

1 As little children, most of us were taught the virtue of honesty from fairy tales and other stories. The story of Pinocchio, who begins life as a <u>puppet</u>, teaches us the importance of telling the truth. The boy who lied by "crying wolf" too many times lost all his sheep as well as the trust of his fellow villagers. In the story of young George Washington, who lied about cutting down the cherry tree, we learn that he earns his father's praise only when he admits what he has done. Even though we know that "honesty is the best policy," why do we often lie in our everyday lives? The fact is that we lie for many reasons.

2 We sometimes lie to minimize our mistakes. While it's true that we all make <u>blunders</u> sometimes, some of us don't have the courage to admit them because we might be blamed for the errors. For example, students might lie to their teachers about unfinished homework. They might say that they left the work at home when, in fact, they didn't even do the work. These students don't want to seem irresponsible, so they make up an excuse—a lie—to save face.

3 Another reason we lie is to get out of situations that we don't want to be in. If we just don't want to attend the dorm meeting early on Saturday morning, we might give this excuse: "I've been fighting off a cold all week, and I need to sleep on Saturday morning, but I'll be sure to attend the next meeting." We lie because we believe that telling the truth will cause problems. We may feel an <u>obligation</u> to maintain good relations with our dormmates. When we don't know how to say no and face whatever problems that may cause, we often use lies to <u>avoid</u> difficulties.

4 However, lies are not always negative; in fact, two kinds of lies can <u>yield</u> positive results. The first is commonly referred to as a "white lie." We tell white lies when we don't want to hurt other people's feelings. For example, if a good friend shows up with an <u>unflattering</u> new haircut, we could be truthful and say, "That haircut looks awful. It doesn't <u>suit</u> you at all!" Instead, we are more likely to lie and say, "I like your haircut. It looks good on you," and spare our friend's feelings. The second kind of positive lie is the "protective lie." This one can help us get out of or avoid dangerous situations. Parents

EXAMPLE ESSAY

often teach their children to use this kind of lie. For example, parents tell their children not to say that they are home alone if they receive phone calls from strangers. In this situation, lying can prevent harm or disaster.

5 People lie for many reasons, both good and bad. However, before we <u>resort to</u> lying to cover up mistakes or to avoid unpleasant situations, perhaps we should rethink our motives for lying. We never know when our lies might be exposed and cause us embarrassment or the loss of people's trust.

puppet: a toy that is moved by strings

blunders: careless mistakes

obligation: a promise or contract

avoid: to keep away from

yield: to produce

unflattering: not favorable

suit: to be appropriate; to fit properly

resort to: to do something only because other options have failed

3. What is the thesis statement?

_____

_____

4. What three examples of liars does the author give in the introduction paragraph?

a. _____

b. _____

c. _____

5. Supporting sentences: In paragraph 4, the author suggests two kinds of lies that can have positive results. What are they?

b. _____

c. _____

6. Reread the concluding paragraph of "Why Do We Lie?" Does the writer offer **a suggestion, an opinion,** or **a prediction**? Circle the appropriate phrase in bold type and write the final sentence from the essay.

_____

_____

_____

DEVELOPING CAUSE-EFFECT ESSAYS

In this next section, you will work on cause-effect essays as you make an outline, write supporting information, study connectors, and choose a topic. Practicing these skills will help you write an effective cause-effect essay.

Activity 2   **Outlining Practice**

The two outlines that follow show causes and effects of teen drug abuse. The first one outlines the causes (focus-on-cause method) and the second one outlines the effects (focus-on-effect method) of teen drug abuse. Complete the outlines with a partner. Use your imagination, knowledge of the topic, and understanding of essay organization. (See Unit 1 for a review of the structure of an essay.) Be sure to notice the thesis statements and use them to help you complete the outlines.

FOCUS-ON-CAUSE OUTLINE

TOPIC: The causes of teenage drug abuse

    I. Introduction (paragraph 1)

        Thesis statement: Teen drug abuse can occur for many reasons, some of which are _____

        _____

        _____

        _____

II. Body

A. Paragraph 2 (cause 1) topic sentence: Teens often begin using drugs because of low self-

esteem.

SUPPORT

    1. Teens are sensitive during adolescence.

    2. Drugs make teens feel powerful.

    3. _____

B. Paragraph 3 (cause 2) topic sentence: _____

_____

SUPPORT

    1. In many families, both parents work outside the home.

    2. Parents often don't have time to pay attention to their children's needs.

    3. Parents may not be aware of the warning signs that their children show.

C. Paragraph 4 (cause 3) topic sentence: _____

_____

SUPPORT

    1. They want to be seen as "cool."

    2. They want to fit into a group.

    3. They want "instant" friends.

III. Conclusion (paragraph 5) (restated thesis): _____

_____

The best way to stop teens from using and abusing drugs is to address all these causes. Only then
will there be a decrease in the number of teenagers who use drugs.

FOCUS-ON-EFFECT OUTLINE

TOPIC: The effects of teenage drug abuse

I. Introduction (paragraph 1)

Thesis statement: When teenagers use drugs, the negative effects can be seen in family relationships, academic performance, and even criminal behavior.

II. Body

A. Paragraph 2 (effect 1) topic sentence: Drug use often leads to a breakdown in family relationships.

> **SUPPORT**
>
> 1. Teens on drugs often stop communicating with parents.
>
> 2. Teens may lie or begin acting strangely at home to protect their drug use.
>
> 3. _____

B. Paragraph 3 (effect 2) topic sentence:

_____

> **SUPPORT**
>
> 1. Students stop caring about schoolwork.
> 2. They may start bothering other kids at school.
> 3. They often skip school to be with their friends who do drugs.

C. Paragraph 4 (effect 3) topic sentence: If teens become addicted to drugs, they will do almost anything, sometimes even commit crimes, to get drugs.

> **SUPPORT**
>
> 1. Drugs are expensive, so teens usually run out of money to buy them.
>
> 2. They might begin stealing from their parents.
>
> 3. _____

III. Conclusion (paragraph 5) (restated thesis): _____

_____

When teens become drug abusers, there are negative consequences not only for the teens themselves but also for their families, friends, and social groups. In the short term, these effects are destructive enough, but they also have long-term effects. Because we look to the young to shape the future of society, we must insure that this future is in good hands. If it is not, societal problems can only get worse.

| Activity 3 | Supporting Information |

The following cause-effect essay is missing the supporting information. As you read the essay, work with a partner to write supporting sentences for each paragraph. If you need more space, use a separate piece of paper. After you finish, compare your supporting information with that of other students.

Essay 16

Did you watch TV when you were a child? In this essay, you provide some facts about children and TV watching.

EXAMPLE ESSAY

Television at Its Worst

1   Mr Stevenson has just come home from a terribly tiring day at work. The first thing he does, after taking off his tie and shoes, is plop down on the couch and turn on the television. Does this sound like a normal routine? It should, because Mr. Stevenson's action is repeated by millions around the world. People use television to relax and to forget about daily troubles. However, what started out decades ago as an exciting, new type of family entertainment is currently being blamed for problems, especially in children. Many researchers now claim that too much television is not good for kids. They have a point; watching too much TV often *does* have negative effects on youngsters.

2   One negative effect of TV on kids is laziness. _____

_____

_____

_____

EXAMPLE ESSAY

3 Another negative point about TV watching is that it may cause children to have

difficulty distinguishing between what's real and what's not. _____

_____

_____

_____

_____

4 A third important effect that television has on kids is that it often desensitizes them

to violence and bad behavior. _____

_____

_____

_____

_____

5 Television has changed over the years to include more and more programs that are
inappropriate for children. For TV to once again play a more positive role in children's
lives, something must be done. Our children's future depends on it.

WRITER'S NOTE: Sequencing Paragraphs

Some writers like to present their strongest or most forceful information in the first
or second paragraphs of an essay. Other writers prefer to end their essays with the
strongest information. Both ways are correct. Choose the sequence of paragraphs that
best presents your information in the way that you want readers to understand it.

LANGUAGE FOCUS: Connectors for Cause-Effect Essays

Connectors show relationships between ideas in sentences and paragraphs. In
cause-effect essays, writers commonly use the connecting words and phrases in the
following lists. (For a more complete list of connectors, see Appendix 3.)

Connectors that show cause:

On account of

As a result of

Because of

Due to

} the rain, we all got wet.

Because

Since

} it rained, we all got wet.

Connectors that show effects:

It rained.

{
For this reason,

Therefore,

As a result,

Thus,

Consequently,
}

we all got wet.

Activity 4   **Connectors**

Read the next student essay (focus-on-effect method) and circle the appropriate connectors in parentheses. Refer to the list in Language Focus if necessary.

Essay 17

Do you use computers in your academic work? Read about how computers have made academic work easier.

Effects of Computers on Higher Education

1   People have always created conveniences to make life easier. One such modern invention is the computer, which has improved many aspects of our lives. One example is in the field of education. (*Therefore/Because of*) computer technology, higher education today has three major conveniences: lecture variety, easy research, and time-saving writing.

2   One important effect of computer technology on higher education is the availability of lectures. (*For this reason/As a result of*) the development of computer networks, we can access lectures from many universities in real time. We are now able to sit down in

front of a digital screen and listen to a lecture being given at another university. In addition, by utilizing interactive media, we can question the lecturer and exchange opinions with other students via e-mail. Such computerized lectures give us access to knowledge that previously we didn't have. (*For this reason/Because*), we can learn from professors in specialized fields, regardless of where they are teaching.

3   The development of computers also makes it possible for us to have access to more information via the Internet and databases. (*Since/Consequently*), when we research a topic, we don't necessarily have to go to the library to find information because the computer has many resources. It is easy to use the Internet and databases since all we have to do is type in a few key words and wait a few moments. In addition, we can do this research at home, making it convenient for busy students.

4   One more effect of computer technology on higher education is time-saving writing techniques. E-mail assignments are becoming more common at universities. (*As a result/ Due to*), the assignments are much quicker and easier to finish than before. When it is time to hand in our assigned papers or homework, we simply send them via e-mail to our professors. This method is beneficial for students and convenient for teachers, who won't risk losing their students' work in a mountain of papers. Another time-saving device is the

EXAMPLE ESSAY

word processor. (*Thus/Because of*) improved word-processing programs, we have the added benefit of spell-checking and grammar-checking programs. If we type a grammatically incorrect sentence, one of these programs highlights the incorrect parts of the sentence and corrects them. In addition, without using a dictionary, we can write papers that have no spelling mistakes. (*Since/As a result of*) these two functions, e-mail and word processing, both teachers and students can save a great deal of time.

5 To summarize, computer technology has three main positive effects on higher education: lecture variety, easy research, and time-saving writing. (*Because of/Because*) the advent of computers in education, we can advance our knowledge and save precious time. Academic life will never be the same!

CHOOSING WORDS CAREFULLY

In all writing, including cause-and-effect essays, attention to precise language is important. Wordiness, or using unnecessary words, is a common problem for many writers. If you can eliminate wordiness from your writing, your essays will be clearer and easier to read.

Wordiness

Some writers think that the more words they use, the better their essay will sound. However, in academic writing in English, it's important to be as concise as possible. Unnecessary words and phrases do not improve your writing. Instead, they make it hard for readers to understand what you want to say.

This list on the left contains common wordy phrases. Try to avoid them in your writing.

Change	To
it goes without saying	(nothing)
at that point in time	at that time
despite the fact that + s + v	despite + noun
for all intents and purposes	(nothing)
in the vicinity of	near
in the final analysis	finally
made a statement saying	said
in the event that	if
the reason why is	because
it seems unnecessary to point out	(nothing)
when all is said and done	(nothing)

Activity 5 | Wordiness

The following introductory paragraph from a cause-effect essay contains six examples of wordy phrases. Underline them as you find them. Then, on separate paper, rewrite the paragraph without the wordy phrases and make it more concise. Note: There is more than one correct way of rewriting this paragraph.

EXAMPLE PARAGRAPH

The fat-free food industry is a tremendous money-making business although recent research has shown that fat-free products are considered only a minor prescription for the purpose of losing weight. Nutritionists have made statements saying that, for all intents and purposes, more important steps to losing weight are exercising and eating well-balanced meals. Despite the fact that this information has appeared, many people still seem to believe that, when all is said and done, eating fat-free food is the best dieting method. The contents of the following essay show some interesting reasons for this fat-free phenomenon.

Redundancy

Redundancy—a kind of wordiness—is the unnecessary repetition of information. When you write, you may want to impress your readers with an eloquent essay that is full of thought-provoking information. One way that writers often try to do this is by loading up on information. You may think, "The more information I have in my essay, the more my readers will enjoy it." This is not usually the case, especially if, instead of adding information, you repeat what you have already said. Repetition can occur in the wording of short phrases as well as in sentences.

Redundant phrases The list on the left contains commonly used redundant phrases. Try to avoid them in your writing. (If you aren't sure why the phrases are redundant, look up the meanings of the two words.)

Change	To
collaborate together	collaborate
completely unanimous	unanimous
courthouse building	courthouse
descend downward	descend
erupt violently	erupt
exactly identical	identical
free gift	gift
merge together	merge
recur again	recur
unexpected surprise	surprise

Redundant sentences The second sentence below contains the same information as the first sentence.

> <u>The United States is the most influential power in the world</u>. Partly because of its abundant material resources and stable political system, <u>this country has great influence in global affairs</u>.

Combine the sentences and eliminate the redundant information.

> The United States has a great influence in global affairs in part because of its abundant material resources and stable political system.

In the next activity, you will practice identifying redundant information.

Activity 6	Don't Say It Twice

Underline the redundant information in this paragraph. Then compare your work with a partner's.

EXAMPLE PARAGRAPH

Many people love to watch science-fiction stories on TV or at the movies. TV shows and films such as *Star Trek* are popular not only because they creatively show how future life might be in three hundred years, but also because they introduce us to characters from other worlds, planets, and galaxies. Perhaps one of the most popular kinds of characters in these futuristic programs is a person with extrasensory perception. ESP is a sense that allows one person to read the mind of another without the exchange of words. These characters, who can read minds and know the innermost thoughts and secrets of other people, often use their gift in less than noble ways. One must remember, however, that these scenes take place in an untrue and fictitious situation. A more interesting concept is to think about what would really happen if ordinary everyday people possessed ESP.

DEVELOPING IDEAS FOR WRITING

Good writers work with ideas that will interest readers. How do writers come up with good ideas? This section will show you some ways to generate ideas for cause-effect essays.

WRITER'S NOTE: Ask Questions

Many writers can think of good topics, but they have trouble developing their topics into essays. One brainstorming method that often helps is to ask questions about the topic (*who? what? where? when? why? how?*). This process often leads to new ideas that can be used in an essay. Especially for a cause-effect essay, good writers ask *why?* This analytical question will exercise your skills in finding cause-and-effect relationships.

Activity 7 **Starting with Questions**

The following questions can all be developed into cause-effect essays. Try to give at least three answers to each question.

1. Why do people gain too much weight?

   _____

   _____

   _____

2. What usually happens after a stock market crash?

   _____

   _____

   _____

3. Why do airplane crashes occur?

   _____

   _____

   _____

4. What would happen if we used a barter system instead of money?

   _____

   _____

   _____

5. What are the causes of _____ ? (Think of your own topic.)

   _____

   _____

   _____

6. What are the effects of _____ ? (Think of your own topic.)

_____

_____

_____

IDEAS

BRAINSTORMING

In the next activity, you will use a brainstorming technique called *clustering*. (See Unit 2 for a review of this technique.) Here is an example of clustering; the topic is the effects of ozone depletion on the environment.

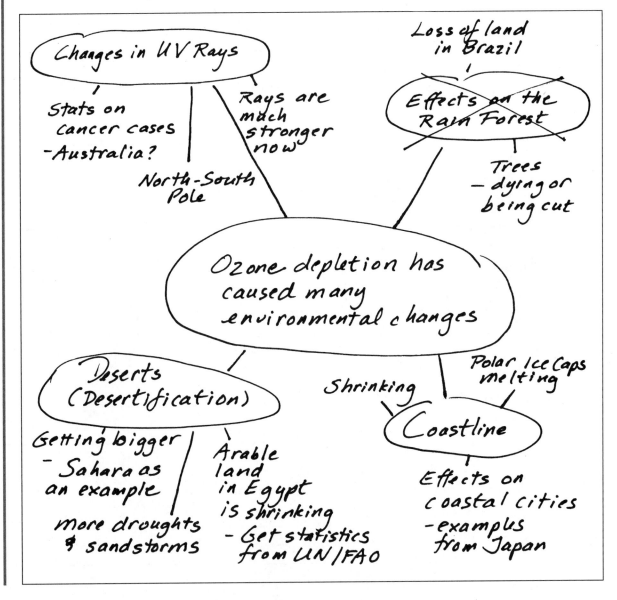

Activity 8 | Clustering Ideas

Choose a topic from Activity 7. With the preceding example as a guide, brainstorm some ideas about your topic using the clustering method. Write all your ideas. When you have finished, cross out the ideas that you don't like or don't want to include in your essay. Explain your brainstorming cluster to a classmate.

Activity 9 | Planning with an Outline

Complete the outline below as a guide to help you brainstorm a more detailed plan for your cause-effect essay. Use your ideas from Activity 8. You may need to use either more or fewer points under each heading. Write in complete sentences where possible.

TOPIC: _____

    I. Introduction (paragraph 1)

        A. Hook: _____

        B. Connecting information: _____

            _____

        C. Thesis statement: _____

            _____

    II. Body

        A. Paragraph 2 (first cause or effect) topic sentence: _____

            _____

SUPPORT

            1. _____

            2. _____

            3. _____

B. Paragraph 3 (second cause or effect) topic sentence: _____

_____

SUPPORT

    1. _____

    2. _____

    3. _____

C. Paragraph 4 (third cause or effect) topic sentence: _____

SUPPORT

    1. _____

    2. _____

    3. _____

III. Conclusion (paragraph 5)

    A. Restated thesis: _____

_____

    B. Suggestion, opinion, or prediction: _____

_____

WRITER'S NOTE: Personal Writing Style

    Some writers work well from an outline and some don't. Some writers write the introduction first, and some write it last. Writing is an individual activity. Use the guidelines in this book and follow whatever process works best for you.

Activity 10   **Peer Editing Your Outline**

Exchange outlines with another student. Read each other's outlines and make comments using the Peer Editing Sheet 5 on page 159.

| Activity 11 | Writing a Cause-Effect Essay |

After you have read your classmate's review of your outline, think about any changes you want to make in your essay. Make sure you have enough information to develop your supporting sentences. Then write your cause-effect essay. Save all your work, including your brainstorming notes, revised drafts, and the Peer Editing Sheet. Be sure to refer to the seven steps in the writing process in Appendix 1 on page 126.

| Activity 12 | Peer Editing Your Essay |

Exchange cause-effect essays from Activity 11 with a partner. Then use Peer Editing Sheet 6 on page 161 to help you comment on your partner's paper. It is important to offer positive comments that will help the writer.

TOPICS FOR WRITING

| Activity 13 | Essay Writing Practice |

Here are more ideas for topics for a cause-effect essay. Before you write, be sure to refer to the seven steps in the writing process in Appendix 1.

1. Children are learning to use computers at a very early age. What are some effects (positive or negative) that computers can have on the intellectual development of children?

2. Going to college is a dream for many people. Some do the work, graduate, and find good jobs. Other students, however, never finish their university studies. Write an essay about what causes students to drop out of college.

3. The United States has the highest divorce rate in the world. Why do you think this is so? Write an essay about what you think are the most common causes of divorce in the United States.

4. The global community is not in agreement about whether cloning is good or bad. What do you think are some possible long-term effects of cloning technology?

5. Many people enjoy traveling and experiencing other cultures. Why do these people feel this way? What causes people to travel outside their native countries?

Unit 5

Argumentative Essays

GOAL: To learn how to write an argumentative essay

LANGUAGE FOCUS: Controlling tone with modals

WHAT IS AN ARGUMENTATIVE ESSAY?

In an argumentative essay, the writer's purpose is to persuade the reader of an opinion about something, for example, that female military personnel can be as effective as male military personnel in combat missions. The writer argues his or her point, gives reasons to support it, and tries to convince the reader.

ARGUING PRO OR CON

Choosing a topic that is appropriate for an argumentative essay is especially important because some things can't be argued. For example, you can't argue that a rose is more beautiful than a daisy—this is an opinion that can't be supported by facts. However, you can argue that roses are more popular than daisies and support the argument with facts about florists' sales of the two kinds of flowers.

Here are a few effective topics and thesis statements for an argumentative essay:

- Marriage under eighteen: People under the age of eighteen should not be allowed to marry.
- Standardized testing: Standardized testing should not be required for application to a university.
- Fast-food restaurants: Communities should decide if fast-food restaurants are right for them.

You can argue either for (pro) or against (con) these statements. If your topic does not have two viewpoints, your essay will not be effective. Look at the following example of an ineffective topic and thesis statement.

Jazz music: Jazz music began with African Americans.

You cannot argue against this statement because it is a fact. Therefore, you cannot write an argumentative essay with this thesis.

WRITER'S NOTE: Choosing a Topic

Be sure that the topic you choose for an argumentative essay can be argued both pro and con.

CONVINCING THE READER

Your job as the writer of an argumentative essay is to convince your readers that your opinion about a topic (your thesis statement) is the most valid viewpoint. To do this, your essay needs to be balanced—it must include an opposing viewpoint, or **counterargument** (see page 110). Even though you are arguing one side of an issue (either for or against), you must think about what someone on the other side of the issue would argue. As soon as you give your opponent's point of view, you must offer a **refutation** of it (see page 110). This means that you refute the other point of view, or show how it is wrong. If you give only your opinion, your essay will sound like propaganda, and your readers will not be convinced of your viewpoint.

EXAMPLE ARGUMENTATIVE ESSAY

A good way to help you learn how to write an argumentative essay is to study an example.

Activity 1   Studying an Example Essay

Read and study the following argumentative essay. Work with a partner to answer the questions before and after the essay. These questions will help you understand the content and the organization of the essay.

Essay 18

In this essay, the writer argues for the use of school uniforms. Do the arguments convince you of the writer's point of view?

1. Did you wear a uniform when you went to school?

2. Some people believe that children are too materialistic these days. For example, they may be too interested in wearing brand-name clothes and shoes. What is your opinion?

The School Uniform Question

EXAMPLE ESSAY

1   Individualism is a <u>fundamental</u> value in the United States. All Americans believe in the right to express their own opinion without fear of punishment. This value, however, is coming under fire in an unlikely place—the public school* classroom. The issue is school uniforms. Should public school students be allowed to make individual decisions about clothing, or should all students be required to wear a uniform? School uniforms are the better choice for three reasons.

2   First, wearing school uniforms would help make students' lives simpler. They would no longer have to decide what to wear every morning, sometimes trying on outfit after outfit in an effort to choose. Uniforms would not only save time but also would eliminate the stress often associated with this chore.

3   Second, school uniforms influence students to act responsibly in groups and as individuals. Uniforms give students the message that school is a special place for learning. In addition, uniforms create a feeling of unity among students. For example, when students do something as a group, such as attend meetings in the auditorium or eat lunch in the cafeteria, the fact that they all wear the same uniform would create a sense of community. Even more important, statistics show the positive effects that

*a school run by the state and paid for in part by property taxes collected in each community

school uniforms have on violence and truancy. According to a recent survey in Hillsborough County, Florida, incidents of school violence dropped by 50 percent, attendance and test scores improved, and student suspensions declined approximately 30 percent after school uniforms were introduced.

4   Finally, school uniforms would help make all the students feel equal. People's standards of living differ greatly, and some people are well-off while others are not. People sometimes forget that school is a place to get an education, not to promote a "fashion show." Implementing mandatory school uniforms would make all the students look the same regardless of their financial status. School uniforms would promote pride and help to raise the self-esteem of students who cannot afford to wear stylish clothing.

5   Opponents of mandatory uniforms say that students who wear school uniforms cannot express their individuality. This point has some merit on the surface. However, as stated previously, school is a place to learn, not to flaunt wealth and fashion. Society must decide if individual expression through clothing is more valuable than improved educational performance. It's important to remember that school uniforms would be worn only during school hours. Students can express their individuality in the way they dress outside of the classroom.

6   In conclusion, there are many well-documented benefits to implementing mandatory school uniforms for students. Studies show that students learn better and act more responsibly when they wear uniforms. Public schools should require uniforms in order to benefit both the students and society as a whole.

fundamental: essential; basic

truancy: absence without permission

well-off: wealthy

implementing: putting into effect

flaunt: to show off; to display

3. The topic of this essay is school uniforms. What is the hook in the first paragraph?

_____

_____

4. What is the thesis statement? _____

_____

5. Topic sentence: Paragraphs 2, 3, and 4 each give a reason for requiring school uniforms. These reasons can be found in the topic sentence of each paragraph. What are the reasons?

Paragraph 2: _____

Paragraph 3: _____

Paragraph 4: _____

6. Supporting sentences: In paragraph 4, what supporting information does the writer give to show that uniforms make students equal?

_____

_____

_____

7. Which paragraph presents a counterargument (an argument that is contrary to, or the opposite of, the writer's opinion)? What is the counterargument?

_____

_____

_____

8. The writer gives a refutation of the counterargument (shows that it is wrong). What is the writer's refutation?

_____

_____

_____

9. Write the sentence from the concluding paragraph of "The School Uniform Question" that restates the thesis.

_____

_____

_____

10. Reread the concluding paragraph. What is the writer's opinion about this issue?

_____

_____

_____

COUNTERARGUMENT AND REFUTATION

The key to persuading the reader that your viewpoint is valid is to support it in every paragraph. While this is not a problem in the first few paragraphs of your essay, the counterargument goes against your thesis statement. This is why every counterargument that you include in your essay needs a refutation. A refutation is a response to the counterargument that disproves it.

Look at the following excerpts from two argumentative essays in this chapter. The counterarguments are in italics and the refutations are underlined.

Essay 18:

Opponents of mandatory uniforms say that students who wear school uniforms cannot express their individuality. This point has some merit on the surface. However, as stated previously, school is a place to learn, not to flaunt wealth and fashion.

Essay 20:

The opponents of capital punishment might say that no one has the right to decide who should die, including the government. However, when the government sends soldiers to war, it is deciding the fate of those soldiers who will die. As long as the government has a right to send its citizens to a battlefield, it has a right to put criminals to death.

As you can see, what begins as a counterargument ends up as another reason in support of your opinion.

WRITER'S NOTE: Arguing Your Point of View

Imagine that you are having an argument with a friend about your topic. He disagrees with your opinion. What do you think will be his strongest argument against your point of view? How will you respond to this counterargument? (Your answer is your refutation.)

DEVELOPING ARGUMENTATIVE ESSAYS

In this next section, you will work on argumentative essays as you make an outline, write supporting information, study modals, and choose a topic.

OUTLINING

Activity 2   **Outlining Practice**

The following outline, which is designed for an argumentative essay, is missing some supporting information. Work with a partner to complete the outline. Use your imagination, knowledge of the topic, and understanding of essay organization to complete this outline with your partner. After you finish, compare your supporting information with that of other students.

TOPIC: Mandatory physical education in school

    I. Introduction (paragraph 1)
       Thesis statement: Physical education classes should be required for all public school students in all grades.

II. Body

    A. Paragraph 2 (pro argument 1) topic sentence: Physical education courses promote children's general health.

SUPPORT

        1. Researchers have proved that exercise has maximum benefit if done regularly.

        2. _____

        3. Students should learn the importance of physical fitness at an early age.

    B. Paragraph 3 (pro argument 2) topic sentence: Physical education teaches children transferable life skills.

SUPPORT

        1. Kids learn about teamwork while playing team sports.

        2. Kids learn about the benefits of healthy competition.

        3. _____

    C. Paragraph 4 (pro argument 3) topic sentence: _____

        _____

SUPPORT

        1. Trained physical education teachers can teach more effectively than parents.

        2. Physical education teachers can usually point a student toward the sport that is more appropriate.

        3. Schools generally have the appropriate facilities and equipment.

    D. Paragraph 5 (counterargument and refutation)

        1. Counterargument: Some parents might disagree and claim that only academic subjects be taught in school.

        2. Refutation: Most parents don't have time or resources to see to it that their children are getting enough exercise. Therefore, it becomes the school's duty to ensure that children are healthy in both mind and body.

III. Conclusion (paragraph 6) (restated thesis): _____

_____ (opinion) Physical education has often

been downplayed as a minor part of daily school life. If its benefits are taken into account and if

schools adopt a twelve-year fitness plan, the positive results will foster a new awareness of not

only physical fitness but also communications skills.

ADDING SUPPORTING INFORMATION

| Activity 3 | Supporting Information |

The following argumentative essay is missing the supporting information. As you read the essay, work with a partner to write supporting sentences for each paragraph. If you need more space, use a separate piece of paper. After you finish, compare your supporting information with that of other students.

Essay 19

Do you know anyone who owns a gun?

Wanted: No Guns!

EXAMPLE ESSAY

1   You hear a noise in the middle of the night. Quickly you reach under the bed. The weapon is in your hand, ready to fire. Bang! You shoot the intruder before he or she can hurt you. In this situation, the "bad guy" was wounded. Sometimes, however, innocent people get hurt or killed by guns. One of the Articles of the Bill of Rights states that citizens of the United States have the "right to bear arms." However, with so many innocent people suffering and dying from accidental shootings, the United States would be much better off if guns were outlawed.

2   The first benefit of making guns illegal is that the number of accidental shootings would decrease.

_____

_____

_____

3   Another benefit of outlawing guns is that the streets would be safer.

_____

_____

_____

4   If guns were illegal, people would be less likely to harm loved ones in moments of anger.

_____

_____

_____

EXAMPLE ESSAY

5 Some people say that they feel safer having a gun at home. However, if guns were more difficult to own, fewer criminals would have them. Fewer guns would lead to a decrease in the number of gun-related crimes and victims.

_____

_____

_____

6 Statistics show that the occurrence of violent crime is much lower in countries that do not allow citizens to carry weapons. Although it is doubtful that the United States would ever completely outlaw the private ownership of weapons, wouldn't it be nice to lower the risk of being shot? It is time for the United States to take a close look at its antiquated gun laws and make some changes for the safety of its citizens.

WRITER'S NOTE: Modals and Tone

Use modals to soften your verbs. For example, change "The president _must_ change his policy." (too strong) to "The president _should_ change his policy" (softer).

LANGUAGE FOCUS: Controlling Tone with Modals

In argumentative essays, good writers are aware of how their arguments sound. Are they too strong? Not strong enough? Certain words can help control the tone of your argument.

Asserting a Point

Strong modals such as _must_, _had better_, and _should_ help writers to assert their main points. When you use these words, readers know where you stand on an issue.

Examples:

The facts clearly show that researchers <u>must</u> stop unethical animal testing.

People who value their health <u>had better</u> stop smoking now.

Public schools <u>should</u> require uniforms in order to benefit both the students and society as a whole.

Acknowledging an Opposing Point

Weaker modals such as _may_, _might_, _could_, _can_, and _would_ help writers make an opposing opinion sound weak. You acknowledge an opposing point when you use _may_, for example, but this weak modal shows that the statement is not strong and can be refuted.

Examples:

While it <u>may</u> be true that people have eaten meat for a long time, the number one killer of Americans now is heart disease, caused in part by the consumption of large amounts of animal fat.

Some Americans <u>may</u> be against legalizing same-sex marriages, but many people were against interracial marriages at first, too.

WRITER'S NOTE: Using Modals for Assertion and for Acknowledging an Opposing View

You are probably already familiar with most of the modals in English—*may, might, can, could, would, must, should, had better, ought to*. Modals can be useful in argumentative essays for two reasons: strong modals help writers make their opinions sound stronger, and weak modals make opposing views sound weaker.

Activity 4	Choosing Modals

Read the following argumentative essay. Underline the modal in parentheses that you feel is most appropriate.

Essay 20

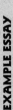
EXAMPLE ESSAY

Life or Death?

1   How would you feel if a loved one were killed? Would you want retribution, or would having the killer in prison be enough? This question has been asked many times, but people are not in agreement about the ultimate punishment. We all know that it is wrong to take a human life, but if our government does the killing, is it still a crime? Some people say that the government doesn't have the right to end someone's life, but the following reasons (*might/will*) show why capital punishment should be preserved.

2   The first reason for allowing the death penalty is for the sake of punishment itself. Most people agree that criminals who commit serious crimes (*might/should*) be separated from society. The punishment (*will/ought to*) depend on the degree of the crime. Capital punishment, the most severe form of punishment, ends criminals' lives. It seems reasonable that this severe punishment be reserved for those who commit the most serious crimes.

3   The second reason to preserve capital punishment is financial. The government (*shouldn't/doesn't*) have to spend a lot of money on criminals. Next to capital punishment, the most severe punishment is a life sentence in prison, where the government (*might/has to*) take care of criminals until they die naturally. These criminals do not work, but they receive free housing and food. It is unfair to use tax dollars for such a purpose.

4   The last reason for continuing the use of the death penalty is based on the purpose of government. If the government has legitimate power to make, judge, and carry out the laws, it (*may/should*) also have the power to decide if criminals should die. Capital punishment is like any other sentence. If one believes that the government has the right to charge a fine or put criminals into jail, then the government (*could/must*) also have the same power to decide the fate of a prisoner's life.

5   The opponents of capital punishment (*must/might*) say that nobody has the right to decide who should die, including the government. However, when the government sends soldiers into war, in some way, it is deciding those soldiers' fate; some will live and some will be killed. As long as the government has a right to send its citizens to a battlefield, it has a right to put criminals to death.

6   There are many good reasons to preserve capital punishment. Certainly not every criminal (*can/should*) be put to death. Capital punishment (*ought to/will*) be viewed as the harshest form of punishment. If no punishment (*can/should*) reform a murderer, then capital punishment is the best thing that can be done for that person and for society.

CHOOSING A TOPIC

Activity 5   Writing Pro and Con Thesis Statements

Read the following list of topics for argumentative essays. For each topic, write a pro (for) thesis statement and a con (against) thesis statement related to the topic. Then compare your statements with your classmates' statements.

Example:

Topic: Women in the military

> Pro thesis statement: In a society where women are chief executive officers of companies, leaders of nations, and family breadwinners, there is no reason why they should not play an active role in the military.

> Con thesis statement: Women should not be allowed to fight in the military because they do not have the strength or endurance required in combat.

1. TOPIC: Using animals in disease research

    Pro thesis statement: _____

    _____

Con thesis statement: _____

_____

2. TOPIC: Homeschooling

Pro thesis statement: _____

_____

Con thesis statement: _____

_____

3. TOPIC: Space exploration

Pro thesis statement: _____

_____

Con thesis statement: _____

_____

4. TOPIC: Smoking in public buildings

Pro thesis statement: _____

_____

Con thesis statement: _____

_____

AVOIDING FAULTY LOGIC

Good writers want to convince readers to agree with their arguments—their reasons and conclusions. If your arguments are not logical, readers won't be convinced. Logic can help prove your point and disprove your opponent's point—and perhaps change a reader's mind about an issue. If you use faulty logic (logic not based on fact), readers will not believe you or take your position seriously.

This section presents a few logical errors that writers sometimes make in argumentative essays. Try to avoid these errors in your writing.

Sweeping Generalizations

Words such as *all*, *always*, and *never* are too broad and can't be supported.

> Example: *All* Americans eat fast food.

> Problem: Maybe every American that you know eats fast food, but the statement that ALL Americans eat it can't be proven.

Events Related Only by Sequence

When one event happens, it doesn't necessarily cause a second event to happen, even if one follows the other in time.

> Example: Henry went to the football game, then he got drunk. Therefore, football games cause drunkenness.

> Problem: The two events may have happened in that order, but don't mislead the reader into thinking that the first action was responsible for the second.

Inappropriate Authority Figures

Using famous names may often help you prove or disprove your point. However, be sure to use the name logically and in the proper context.

> Example: Madonna is a good singer. As a result, she would make a good orchestra conductor.

> Problem: While Madonna may be a good singer, this quality will not necessarily make her a good orchestra conductor.

Hasty Generalizations

Hasty generalizations are just what they sound like—making quick judgments based on inadequate information. This kind of logical fallacy is a common error in argumentative writing.

> Example: Joe didn't want to study at a university. Instead, he decided to go to a technical school. He is now making an excellent salary repairing computers. Bill doesn't want to study at a university. Therefore, he should go to a technical school to become financially successful.

> Problem: While Joe and Bill have something in common (they don't want to study at a university), this fact alone does not mean that Bill would be successful doing the same thing that Joe did. Other information may be important as well, such as the fact that Joe has lots of experience with computers or that Bill has problems with manual dexterity.

Loaded Words

Some words contain positive or negative connotations. Try to avoid them when you make an argument.

> Example: The blue-flag *freedom fighters* won the war against the green-flag *guerrillas*.

Problem: The words *freedom fighters* (positive) and *guerrillas* (negative) may bias readers about the two groups without any support for the bias.

Either/Or Arguments

When you argue a point, be careful not to limit the choices to only two or three.

Example: The instructor must either return the tests or dismiss the class.

Problem: This statement implies that only two choices are available to the instructor.

Activity 6   **Faulty Logic**

Read the following paragraph and underline all the uses of faulty logic. Write the kind of error above the words.

Next week our fine upstanding citizens will go to the polls to vote for or against a penny sales tax for construction of a new stadium. This law, if passed, will cause extreme hardship for local residents. Our taxes are high enough as it is, so why do our city's apathetic leaders think that we will run happily to the polls and vote YES? If we take a look at what happened to our sister city as a result of a similar bill, we will see that this new tax will have negative effects. Last year that city raised its sales tax by 1 percent. Only three weeks later, the city was nearly destroyed by a riot in the streets. If we want to keep our fair city as it is, we must either vote NO on the ballot question or live in fear of violence.

IDEAS BRAINSTORMING

Brainstorming will help you get started with your argumentative essay. In this section, you will choose any method of brainstorming that works for you and develop supporting information.

Activity 7 — Choosing a Topic

1. First, choose a thesis from the statements that you wrote in Activity 5 on pages 116–117 or choose any other topic and thesis statement that you want to write about. Remember that the topic must have more than one point of view to qualify as an argument.

   Essay topic: _____

   Thesis statement: _____

   _____

2. Now brainstorm about your topic. Write everything you can think of that supports your argument. Use clustering, diagramming, or another method of brainstorming. You may want to begin by answering this question about your thesis statement: *Why do I believe this?*

3. Look at your brainstorming information again. Choose three or four reasons that support your thesis *most effectively* and circle them. You now know what your major supporting information will be.

4. Now that you have written your thesis and a few reasons to support it, it's time to give attention to opposing points of view. On the lines below, write one counterargument and a refutation for your argumentative essay.

   Counterargument: _____

   _____

   _____

   Refutation: _____

   _____

   _____

   Remember that in your conclusion, you should include a restatement of the thesis and your opinion about the issue.

Activity 8 — Planning with an Outline

Complete the outline on page 121 as a guide to help you brainstorm a more detailed plan for your argumentation essay. Use your ideas from Activity 7 (above). You may need to use either more or fewer points under each heading. Write complete sentences where possible.

Description of Score Points Used in Evaluating the TASP Test Writing Sample

Score Point	Description of Writing Sample
4 —	**a well-formed writing sample that effectively communicates a whole message to a specified audience** The writer maintains unity of a developed topic throughout the writing sample and establishes a focus by clearly stating a purpose. The writer exhibits control in the development of ideas and clearly specifies supporting detail. Sentence structure is effective and free of errors. Choice of words is precise, and usage is careful. The writer shows mastery of mechanical conventions, such as spelling and punctuation.
3 —	**an adequately formed writing sample that attempts to communicate a message to a specified audience** The focus and the purpose of the writing sample may be clear; however, the writer's attempts to develop supporting details may not be fully realized. The writer's organization of ideas may be ambiguous, incomplete, or partially ineffective. Sentence structure within paragraphs is adequate, but minor errors in sentence structure, usage, and word choice are evident. There may also be errors in the use of mechanical conventions, such as spelling and punctuation.
2 —	**a partially developed writing sample in which the characteristics of effective written communication are only partially formed** The statement of purpose is not clear, and, although a main idea or topic may be announced, focus on the main idea is not sustained. Ideas may be developed by the use of specific supporting detail, and the writer may make an effort to organize and sequence ideas, but development and organization are largely incomplete or unclear. Paragraphs contain poorly structured sentences with noticeable and distracting errors. The writer exhibits imprecision in usage and word choice and a lack of control of mechanical conventions, such as spelling and punctuation.
1 —	**an inadequately formed writing sample that fails to communicate a complete message** The writer attempts to address the topic, but language and style may be inappropriate for the given audience, purpose, and/or occasion. There is often no clear statement of a main idea and the writer's efforts to present supporting detail are confused. Any organization that is present fails to present an effective sequence of ideas. Sentence structure is ineffective and few sentences are free of errors. Usage and word choice are imprecise. The writer makes many errors in the use of mechanical conventions, such as spelling and punctuation.

Note: A score of U is given if the writing sample is off topic, illegible, primarily in a language other than English, or not of a sufficient length to score. A score of B is used if the writing sample is completely blank (i.e., the examinee made no response to the writing assignment).

SYLLABUS FOR ARGUMENTATION ESSAY

Week	Day	Hour	Lesson	Text Reference & needed materials	Homework
13	T	1	**DAR: Introduction to TASP: History, structure and nature of grading.**	TASP reference: rubric for grading	Read rubric and be prepared to apply it.
13	T	2	*HVL: Introduction to argumentation: Read and discuss essay on Pg. 107; focus on basic structure of essay: Introduction + proposition + thesis + arguments + refutation*	*Great Essays, Pgs. 107 – 108*	*Questions on Pg. 108-109 (# 's 3-10)*
13	Th	1	**DAR: Basic structure of argumentation; Introduction to Toulmin model of argumentation**	Toulmin handouts	
13	Th	2	*HVL: Application of Toulmin model: Using Toulmin model on essay on Pg. 107-108*	Toulmin worksheet	Activity #3, Pg. 113-114
14	T	1	**DAR: Group reading of TASP sample essays and discussion of them.**	TASP rubric and sample essays.	
14	T	2	*HVL:*		
14	Th	1	*THANKSGIVING*		
14	Th	2			
15	T	1	**DAR: Group activity for brainstorming arguments for & against propositions.**	Topic and brainstorming and outline sheets	
15	T	2	HVL: In-class brainstorming for argumentative essay		
15	Th	1	In-Class Essay: Drafting	Composition sheets	
15	Th	2	" " " "		

TOPIC: _____

   I. Introduction (paragraph 1)

     A. Hook: _____

     B. Connecting information: _____

        _____

     C. Thesis statement: _____

        _____

  II. Body

     A. Paragraph 2 (first reason) topic sentence: _____

        _____

SUPPORT

        1. _____

        2. _____

        3. _____

     B. Paragraph 3 (second reason) topic sentence: _____

        _____

SUPPORT

        1. _____

        2. _____

        3. _____

     C. Paragraph 4 (third reason) topic sentence: _____

        _____

SUPPORT

        1. _____

        2. _____

        3. _____

D. Paragraph 4 (counterargument and refutation)

SUPPORT

1. Counterargument: _____

_____

2. Refutation: _____

_____

III. Conclusion (paragraph 5)

A. Restated thesis: _____

_____

B. Opinion: _____

_____

Activity 9   Peer Editing Your Outline

Exchange outlines with another student. Read each other's outlines and make comments using Peer Editing Sheet 7 on page 163.

Activity 10   Writing an Argumentative Essay

After you have read your classmate's review of your outline, think about any changes you want to make in your essay. Make sure you have enough information to develop your supporting sentences. Then write your argumentative essay. Save all your work, including your brainstorming notes, revised drafts, and the Peer Editing Sheet. Be sure to refer to the seven steps in the writing process in Appendix 1 on page 126.

Activity 11   Peer Editing Your Essay

Exchange argumentation essays from Activity 10 with a partner. Then use Peer Editing Sheet 8 on page 165 to help you comment on your partner's paper. It is important to offer positive comments that will help the writer.

TOPICS FOR WRITING

Activity 12	Essay Writing Practice

Here are more ideas for topics for an argumentative essay. Before you write, be sure to refer to the seven steps in the writing process in Appendix 1.

1. The media often place heavy emphasis on the opinions and actions of celebrities such as actors and sports stars. Should we pay attention to these opinions and actions? Are they important or not? Choose one side and write your essay in support of it.

2. At what age should a person be considered an adult? Make a decision about this issue, then argue your point of view. Don't forget to include a counterargument and refutation.

3. Consider the issue of assisted suicide for terminally ill people. Do you think it should be allowed? Argue one side or the other of this issue.

4. Should a passing TOEFL score be the main requirement for international students to enter a university? What are the pros and cons of this issue? Choose one side and write your essay in support of it.

5. Is daycare beneficial for children under the age of five? Should one parent stay home with children for the first few years of life? Develop a thesis statement about some aspect of the daycare versus home care issue and support it in your argumentative essay.

Part II

Appendices

Unit 4, Activity 10: Cause-Effect Essay Outline

Unit 4, Activity 12: Cause-Effect Essay

Unit 5, Activity 9: Argumentative Essay Outline

Unit 5, Activity 11: Argumentative Essay

Appendix 5 Answer Key

Appendix 1

Understanding the Writing Process: The Seven Steps

This section can be read at any time during the course. You will want to refer to these seven steps many times as you write your essays.

THE ASSIGNMENT

Imagine that you have been given the following assignment: *Write an essay in which you discuss the benefits or problems of vegetarianism.* What should you do first? What should you do second, and so on? There are many ways to write, but most good writers follow certain general steps in the writing process. These steps are guidelines that are not always followed in order.

Look at this list of steps. Which ones do you do? Which ones have you never done?

1. Choosing a topic
2. Brainstorming
3. Outline and rough draft
4. Cleaning up the rough draft
5. Peer editing
6. Revising the draft
7. Proofing the final paper

Next you will see how one student, Sean, went through the steps to do the assignment. First, read the final essay that Sean gave his teacher.

Essay 21

Better Living as a Vegetarian

I   The hamburger is an American cultural icon that is known all over the world. Eating meat, especially beef, is an integral part of daily life for a majority of people in the United States. The consumption of large quantities of meat is a major contributing factor toward a great many deaths in this country, including the unnecessarily high number of deaths

EXAMPLE WRITING

from heart-related problems. Though it has caught on slowly in this culture, vegetarianism is a way of life that can help improve not only the quality of people's lives but also their longevity.

2   Surprising as it may sound, vegetarianism can have beneficial effects on the environment. Because demand for meat animals is so high, cattle are being raised in areas where rain forests once stood. As rain forest land is cleared in order to make room for cattle ranches, the environmental balance is upset. This could have serious consequences for humans. Studies show that much of the current global warming is due to disturbing the rain forests.

3   More important at an individual level is the question of how eating meat affects a person's health. Meat, unlike vegetables, can contain very large amounts of fat. Eating this fat has been connected in research cases with certain kinds of cancer. If people cut down on the amounts of meat they ate, they would automatically be lowering their risks of disease. Furthermore, eating animal fat can lead to obesity, and obesity can cause numerous health problems. For example, obesity can cause people to slow down and their heart to have to work harder. This results in high blood pressure. Meat is also high in cholesterol, and this only adds to health problems. With so much fat consumption in this country, it is no wonder that heart disease is a leading killer of Americans.

4   If people followed vegetarian diets, their health would improve. In fact, it could even save someone's life. Eating certain kinds of vegetables, such as broccoli, brussels sprouts, and cauliflower, has been shown to reduce the chance of contracting colon cancer later in life. Vegetables do not contain the "bad" fats that meat does. Vegetables do not contain cholesterol, either. Furthermore, native inhabitants of areas of the world where people eat more vegetables than meat, notably certain areas of the former Soviet Asian republics, routinely live to be over one hundred.

5   Some people argue that, human nature being what it is, it would be unhealthy for humans to not eat meat. They say that humans are naturally carnivores and cannot help wanting to consume a juicy piece of red meat. However, anthropologists have shown that early humans ate meat only when other foods were not abundant. Man is inherently an herbivore, not a carnivore.

6   Numerous scientific studies have shown the benefits of vegetarianism for people in general, and I know firsthand how my life has improved since I decided to give up meat entirely. Though it was difficult at first, I have never regretted my decision to become a vegetarian. I feel better, and my friends tell me that I look better than ever before. More and more people are becoming aware of the risks associated with meat consumption. If you become vegetarian, your life will improve, too.

STEPS IN THE WRITING PROCESS

STEP 1: CHOOSING A TOPIC

For this assignment, the topic was given: the benefits or problems of vegetarianism. As you consider the assignment, you have to decide what kind of essay to write. Will you compare or contrast the benefits of vegetarianism with another type of diet? Will you talk about the causes and effects of vegetarianism? Will you argue that vegetarianism is or is not better than eating animal products?

Sean chose to write an argumentative essay about vegetarianism to try to convince readers of its benefits.

STEP 2: BRAINSTORMING

The next step for Sean was to brainstorm.

In this step, you write every idea that pops into your head about your topic. Some of these ideas will be good, and some will be bad; write them all. The main purpose of brainstorming is to write as many ideas as you can think of. If one idea looks especially good, you might circle that idea or put a check next to it. If you write an idea and you know right away that you are not going to use it, you can cross it out.

Brainstorming methods include making lists, clustering (see Unit 2), and diagramming (see Unit 3). Use whatever method you like best.

Look at Sean's brainstorming diagram on the topic of vegetarianism.

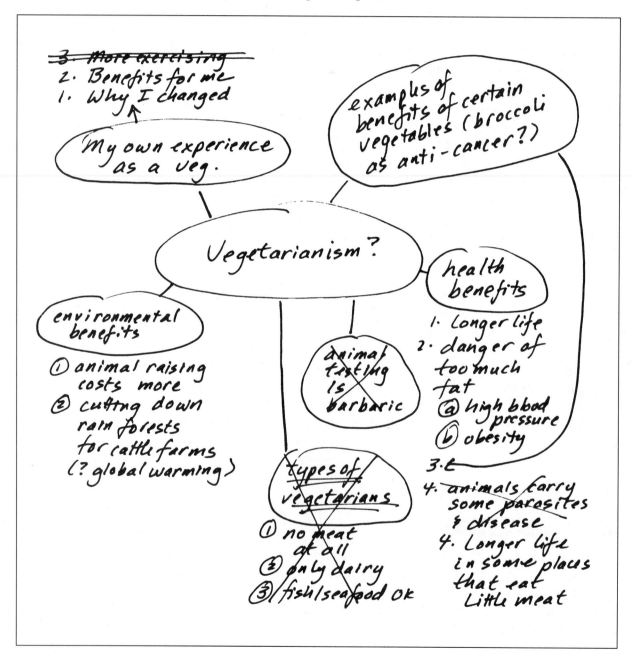

Sean's brainstorming diagram

As you can see from the brainstorming diagram, Sean considered many benefits of being a vegetarian. Notice a few items in the diagram. As he organized his brainstorming, Sean wrote "examples of benefits of certain vegetables" as a spoke on the wheel. Then he realized that this point would be a good number 3 in the list of benefits, so he drew an arrow to show that he should move it there. For number 4, Sean wrote "animal testing for cosmetics." Then he decided that this is not related to the topic of the benefits of becoming a vegetarian, so he crossed it out.

Getting the Information

How would you get the information for this brainstorming exercise?

- You might read a book or an article about vegetarianism.

- You could spend time in a library looking for articles on the subject.

- You could also interview an expert on the topic, such as a vegetarian or a nutritionist. This method is not only useful but also fun. You can ask the person specific questions about parts of the topic that are not clear to you.

WRITER'S NOTE: Do Research

To get information and develop your thoughts about your essay topic, you may need to do some research.

STEP 3: OUTLINE AND ROUGH DRAFT

This step has two parts: an outline and a rough draft.

Outline

Next, create an outline for the essay. Here is Sean's rough outline that he wrote from his brainstorming notes.

I. Introduction
  a. Define vegetarianism
  b. List different types

  c. Thesis statement: _____

II. Environmental benefits
  a. Rain forests
  b. Global warming

III. Health issues

    a. Too much fat from meat → obesity → diseases → cancer

    b. High blood pressure and heart disease

    c. Cancer-fighting properties of broccoli and cauliflower, etc.

IV. Counterargument

    a. Man is carnivore?

    b. Not true

V. Conclusion

    Opinion: life will improve

After you have chosen the main points for your essay, you will need to develop some supporting details. You should include examples, reasons, explanations, definitions, or personal experiences. One of the most common techniques in generating these supporting details is asking specific questions about the topic, for example:

SUPPORT

What is it?

What happened?

How did this happen?

What is it like or not like? Why?

Rough Draft

Next, Sean wrote a rough draft. In this step you take information from your brainstorming session and write the essay. This first draft may contain many errors, such as misspellings, incomplete ideas, and comma errors. At this point, don't worry about correcting the errors. The main thing is to put your ideas into sentences.

You may feel that you don't know what you think about the topic yet. In this case, it may be difficult for you to write, but it's important to just write, no matter what comes out. Sometimes writing helps you think, and as soon as you form a new thought, you can write it.

Making changes As you write the rough draft, you may want to add information or take some out. In some cases, your rough draft may not follow your outline exactly. That is okay. Writers don't always stick with their original plan or follow the steps in the writing process in order. Sometimes they go back and forth between steps. The writing process is much more like a cycle than a line.

Read Sean's rough draft with his teacher's comments.

Better Living as a Vegetarian

Wow — too abrupt? You don't talk about hamburgers any more??

(Do you like hamburgers?) Eating meat, especially beef, is an interesting part of the daily *vocabulary?*

life in the United States. In addition, this high eating of meat is a major contributing thing *factor* *word choice?*

causes
that makes a great many deaths in this country, including the unnecessarily high number

of deaths from heart-related problems. Vegetarianism has caught on slowly in this culture.

) and it
Vegetarianism is a way of life that can help improve not only the quality of people's lives but

also people's longevity. → *the quality but also the length of people's lives*

This is not a topic sentence
Because demand for meat animals is so high, Cattle are being raised in areas where the

rain forest once stood. As rain forest land is cleared in massive amounts in order to make

room for the cattle ranches, the environmental balance is being upset. This could have

For example,   *transition?*
serious consequences for us in both the near and long term. How much of the current global

warming is due to man's disturbing the rain forest?
You need a more specific topic relating to health.

(Meat contains a high amount of fat.) Eating this fat has been connected in research

cases with certain kinds of cancer. Furthermore, eating animal fat can lead to obesity, and

obesity can cause many different kinds of diseases, for example, obesity can cause people to

slow down and their heart to have to word harder. This results in high blood pressure.

Meat is high in cholesterol, and this only adds to the health problems. With the high

consumption of animal fat in this country, it is no wonder that heart disease is a leading

killer of Americans.

On the other hand, eating a vegetarian diet can improve a person's health. And

Sean's rough draft

necessary?

vegetables taste so good. In fact, it can even save someone's life. Eating certain kinds of

vegetables such as broccoli, brussel sprouts, and cauliflower has been shown to reduce the

combine sentences?

chance of having colon cancer later in life. Vegetables do not contain the "bad" fats that

meat does. Vegetables do not contain cholesterol, either. Native inhabitants of areas of the

world where mostly vegetables are consumed, notably certain areas of the former Soviet

Asian republics, routinely live to be over one hundred. — *A Where's the counter argument and refutation*

good sentence Though numerous scientific studies have shown the benefits of vegetarianism for people

in general, I know first-hand how my life has improved since I decided to give up meat

entirely. In 1994, I saw a TV program that discussed problems connected to animals that are

raised for food. The program showed how millions of chickens are raised in dirty, crowded — *not related to your topic*

conditions until they are killed. The program also talked about how diseases can be spread

from cow or pig to humans due to unsanitary conditions. Shortly after I saw this show, I

decided to try life without eating meat. Though it was difficult at first, I have never regretted

my decision to become a vegetarian. I feel better and my friends tell me that I look better

than ever before

Being a vegetarian has many benefits. Try it.   — *This is too short! How about making a prediction or suggestion for the reader. The previous paragraph told how the writer became a vegetarian, so doesn't it make sense for the conclusion to say something like "I'm sure your life will be better too if you become a vegetarian?"*

I like this essay. You really need to work on the conclusion.

Rough draft tips   Here are some things to remember about the rough draft copy:

- The rough draft is not the final copy. Even native speakers who are good writers do not write an essay only one time. They rewrite as many times as necessary until the essay is the best that it can be.

- It's okay for you to make notes on your drafts, circle words, draw connecting lines, cross out words, write new information. Make notes to yourself about what to change, what to add, or what to reconsider.

- If you can't think of a word or an idea as you write, leave a blank space or circle. Then go back and fill in the space later. If you write a word that you know isn't the right one, circle or underline it so you can fill in the right word later. Don't stop writing. When people read your draft, they can see these areas you are having trouble with and offer comments that may help.

- Don't be afraid to throw some sentences away if they don't sound right. Just as a good housekeeper throws away unnecessary things from the house, so a good writer throws out unnecessary or wrong words or sentences.

STEP 4: CLEANING UP THE ROUGH DRAFT

The handwriting in the first draft is usually not neat. Sometimes it's so messy that only the writer can read it! Use a word processor, if possible, to make writing and revising easier.

After you make notes on your rough draft, put it away for several hours or a few days. You may find it helpful to come back to the paper later when you are fresh and are more likely to see problems. At that time, copy the draft again in a neater hand or type it on a computer, if you have one. If you notice any words or sentences that don't belong, throw them out. At this time you may also want to add ideas that make the paper better.

STEP 5: PEER EDITING

Sean used Peer Editing Sheet 8 to get feedback on his essay draft. Peer editing is important in the writing process. You don't always see your own mistakes or places where information is missing because you are too close to the essay that you created. Ask someone to read your draft and give you feedback about your writing. Choose someone that you trust and feel comfortable with. Some people feel uneasy about peer editing, but the result is almost always a better essay. Remember to be polite when you edit another student's paper.

STEP 6: REVISING THE DRAFT

This step consists of three parts:

1. Reacting to the comments on the peer editing sheet

2. Rereading the essay and making changes

3. Rewriting the essay one more time

STEP 7: PROOFING THE FINAL PAPER

Most of the hard work is over now. In this step, the writer pretends to be a brand-new reader who has never seen the essay before. Proofread your essay for grammar, punctuation, and spelling errors and to see if the sentences flow smoothly.

Read Sean's final paper again on pages 126–127.

Of course, the very last step is to turn the paper in to your teacher and hope that you get a good grade!

WRITER'S NOTE: Proofread

One good way to proofread your essay is to first set it aside for several hours or a day or two. The next time you read your essay, your head will be clearer and you will be more likely to see any problems.

Appendix 2

Additional Grammar Practice

The three essays in this section feature different grammatical errors. Each paragraph highlights one kind of error. In each case, read the entire essay before you complete the practices.

Essay 22

Remember to read the whole essay first. Then go back and complete each practice.

Practice 1   *Verb Forms*

Read the paragraph and decide whether the five underlined verbs are correct. If not, draw a line through the verb and write the correct form above the verb.

A Simple Recipe

EXAMPLE WRITING

1   "When in Rome, do as the Romans do" may <u>sound</u> ridiculous, but this proverb <u>offer</u> an important suggestion. If you travel to other countries, especially to a country that <u>is</u> very different from your own, you should <u>keeping</u> this saying in mind. For example, Japan has unique customs that <u>is</u> not found in any other country. If you <u>traveled</u> to Japan, you should find out about Japanese customs, taboos, and people beforehand.

Practice 2   *Verb Forms*

Read this paragraph carefully. Then write the correct form of the verbs in parentheses.

2 One custom is that you should (take) _____ off your shoes before (enter) _____ someone's house. In Japan, the floor must always be kept clean because usually people (sit) _____ , eat a meal, or even (sleep) _____ on the floor. Another custom is giving gifts. The Japanese often (give) _____ a small gift to people who have (do) _____ favors for them. Usually this token of gratitude (give) _____ in July and December to keep harmonious relations with the receiver. When you (give) _____ someone such a gift, you should make some form of apology about it. For example, many Japanese will say, "This is just a small gift that I have for you." In addition, it is not polite to open a gift immediately. The receiver usually (wait) _____ until the giver has left so the giver will not be embarrassed if the gift (turn) _____ out to be defective or displeasing.

Practice 3   *Connectors*

Read the paragraph carefully. Then fill in the blanks with one of these connectors:

because	in addition
even if	for example
first	but

EXAMPLE WRITING

3 _____ , it is important to know about Japanese taboos. All cultures have certain actions that are considered socially unacceptable. _____ something is acceptable in one culture, it can easily be taboo in another culture. _____ , chopsticks are used in many cultures, _____ there are two taboos about chopsticks etiquette in Japan. _____ , you should never stand the chopsticks upright in your bowl of rice. _____ standing chopsticks upright is done at a funeral ceremony, this action is associated with death. Second, you must never pass food from one pair of chopsticks to another. Again, this is related to burial rites in Japan.

Practice 4   *Articles*

There are fourteen blanks in this paragraph. Read the paragraph and write the articles a, an, or the to complete the sentences. Some blanks do not require articles.

EXAMPLE WRITING

4   Third, it is important to know that Japanese people have _____ different cultural values. One of _____ important differences in _____ cultural values is _____ Japanese desire to maintain _____ harmony at all costs. People try to avoid causing any kind of dispute. If there is _____ problem, both sides are expected to compromise in order to avoid an argument. People are expected to restrain their emotions and put _____ goal of compromise above their individual wishes. Related to this is _____ concept of patience. Japanese put _____ great deal of _____ value on _____ patience. Patience also contributes to maintaining _____ good relations with _____ everyone and avoiding _____ disputes.

Practice 5   *Prepositions*

Read this paragraph and write the correct preposition in each blank. Choose from these prepositions: into, in, to, about, with, of, around. *You may use them more than once.*

6 _____ conclusion, if you want to get along well _____

the Japanese and avoid uncomfortable situations when you go _____ Japan,

it is important to take _____ account the features _____

Japanese culture that have been discussed here. Though it may be hard to understand

Japanese customs because they are different, knowing _____ them can help

you adjust to life in Japan. If you face an unfamiliar or difficult situation when you are

_____ Japan, you should do what the people _____ you do.

In other words, "When _____ Japan, do as the Japanese do."

Essay 23

Remember to read the whole essay first. Then go back and complete each practice.

Practice 1   *Verb Forms*

Read this paragraph carefully. Then write the correct form of the verbs in parentheses.

Corporal Punishment Is Wrong

1 What should parents do when their five-year-old child says a bad word even though

the child knows it is wrong? What should a teacher (do) _____ when a

student in the second grade (call) _____ the teacher a name? When my

parents (be) _____ children forty or fifty years ago, the answer to these

questions was quite clear. The adult would spank the child immediately. Corporal

punishment (be) _____ quite common then. When I was a child, I (be)

_____ in a class in which the teacher got angry at a boy who kept (talk) _____ after she told him to be quiet. The teacher then (shout)

_____ at the boy and, in front of all of us, (slap) _____ his

face. My classmates and I were shocked. Even after twenty years, I still remember that

incident quite clearly. If the teacher's purpose (be) _____ to (teach)

_____ us to (be) _____ quiet, she did not (succeed)

_____ . However, if her purpose was to create an oppressive mood in the

class, she succeeded. Because corporal punishment (be) _____ an

ineffective and cruel method of discipline, it should never (use) _____

under any circumstances.

Practice 2   *Prepositions*

Read this paragraph carefully. Write the correct preposition in each blank. Use these prepositions: in, of, for.

2 Supporters _____ corporal punishment claim that physical discipline is necessary

_____ developing a child's sense _____ personal responsibility. Justice Powell, a

former U.S. Supreme Court justice, has even said that paddling children who misbehave

has been an acceptable method _____ promoting good behavior and responsibility

_____ school children for a long time. Some people worry that stopping corporal

punishment in schools could result _____ a decline _____ school achievement.

However, just because a student stops misbehaving does not mean that he or she

suddenly has a better sense _____ personal responsibility or correct behavior.

Practice 3   *Articles*

Read the paragraph and write the articles a, an, or the to complete the sentences. Some blanks do not require articles.

EXAMPLE WRITING

3 Corporal punishment is _____ ineffective way to punish _____ child because it may stop a behavior for a while, but it will not necessarily have _____ long-term effect. Thus, if an adult inflicts _____ mild form of _____ corporal punishment that hurts the child very little or not at all, it will not get rid of the bad behavior. Moreover, because corporal punishment works only temporarily, it will have to be repeated whenever the child misbehaves. It may then become _____ standard response to any misbehavior. This can lead to _____ frequent and more severe spanking, which may result in _____ abuse.

Practice 4   *Comma Splices*

Read this paragraph carefully and find the two comma splices. Correct them in one of two ways: (1) change the comma to a period and make two sentences, or (2) add a connector after the comma.

EXAMPLE WRITING

4 A negative effect of corporal punishment in school is that it makes some students feel aggressive toward parents, teachers, and fellow students. In my opinion, children regard corporal punishment as a form of teacher aggression that makes them feel helpless. Therefore, students may get frustrated if corporal punishment is used frequently. Furthermore, it increases disruptive behavior that can become more aggressive, this leads to school violence and bullying of fellow students. Supporters of corporal punishment believe that it is necessary to maintain a good learning environment, it is unfortunate that the opposite result often happens. The learning environment actually becomes less effective when there is aggressive behavior.

Practice 5   *Verb Forms*

Read the paragraph and decide whether the underlined verbs are correct. If not, draw a line through the verb and write the correct form above it.

5 Last, corporal punishment may <u>result</u> in antisocial behavior later in life because it teaches children that adults <u>condone</u> violence as a solution to problems. Children who <u>spank</u> learn that it is acceptable for a stronger person <u>using</u> violence against a weaker person. The concept of "might makes right" is <u>forced</u> upon them at a very early age. Furthermore, this concept <u>teaches</u> a lesson not only to those who are spanked but also to those who <u>witness</u> it. Studies of prisoners and delinquents <u>shows</u> that nearly 100 percent of the violent inmates at San Quentin and 64 percent of juvenile delinquents <u>was</u> victims of seriously abusive punishment during childhood. If serious punishment <u>causes</u> antisocial behavior, perhaps even milder punishment also <u>contribute</u> to violence. Research at the University of New Hampshire <u>will find</u> that children who were spanked between the ages of three and five <u>showed</u> higher levels of antisocial behavior when they <u>observed</u> just two and four years later. This behavior included higher levels of beating family members, hitting fellow students, and defying parents. It is ironic that the behaviors for which teachers <u>punishing</u> students often get worse as a result of the spanking.

Practice 6   *Editing for Errors*

There are seven errors in this paragraph. They are in word forms (2), articles (1), sentence fragments (1), verb tense (1), and subject-verb agreement (2). Mark these errors and write corrections.

6 For punishment to be effective, it must produce a great behavioral change, result in behavior that is permanent, and produce minimal side effects. However, none of these changes is a result of corporal punishment. Therefore, we should consider alternatives to corporal punishment. Because discipline is necessary to educate children. One of the alternatives are to emphasize students' positive behaviors. Some research shows that

EXAMPLE WRITING

reward, praise, and self-esteem is the most powerful motivators for the learning. Other alternatives are to hold conferences with students to help them plan acceptable behave or to use school staff such as psychologists and counselors. It is important to build better interpersonal relations between teachers and students. In addition to these alternatives, instruction that reaches all students, such as detention, in-school suspension, and Saturday school, is available to discipline and punishment unruly students, too. Alternatives to corporal punishment taught children to be self-disciplined rather than to be cooperative only because of fear.

Practice 7   *Editing for Errors*

There are seven errors in this paragraph. They are in word forms (1), articles (3), sentence fragments (1), comma splices (1), and subject-verb agreement (1). Mark these errors and write the corrections.

EXAMPLE ESSAY

7 In the conclusion, teachers should not use corporal punishment because it is ineffective in disciplining students and may have long-term negative effects on students. Moreover, teachers should not forget that love and understanding must be part of any kind of discipline. Discipline and love is not opposites, punishment must involve letting the children know that what they do is wrong and why punishment is necessary. Teachers should not just beat student with the hopeful that he will understand. It is important to maintain discipline without inflicting physical pain on students. Therefore, teachers should use effective and more humane alternatives. In order to bring about permanent behavioral changes.

Essay 24

Remember to read the whole essay first. Then go back and complete each practice.

Practice 1   *Articles*

Read the paragraph and write the articles a, an, *or the to complete the sentences. Some blanks do not require articles.*

Washington and Lincoln

EXAMPLE WRITING

I Perhaps no other names from _____ American history are better known than the

names of George Washington and Abraham Lincoln. _____ Both of these presidents

made valuable contributions to _____ United States during their presidency. In fact,

one could argue that _____ America would not be _____ same country that it is

today if either of these two leaders had not been involved in _____ American politics.

However, it is interesting to note that though both leaders made _____ significant

contributions to _____ country, they lived in _____ quite different times and

served in _____ very different ways.

Practice 2   *Verb Forms*

Read this paragraph carefully. Then write the correct form of the verbs in parentheses.

EXAMPLE WRITING

2 Everyone (know) _____ that George Washington was the first president

of the United States. What most people do not (appreciate) _____ (be)

_____ that Washington (be) _____ a clever military leader. He

served the country in the early days of the revolution by (help) _____ to

change the colonial volunteers from ragged farmers into effective soldiers. Without

Washington's bravery and military strategy, it is doubtful that the colonies could have

(beat) _____ the British. Thus, without Washington, the colonies might

never even have (become) _____ the United States of America.

Practice 3   *Prepositions*

Read this paragraph and write the correct preposition in each blank. Choose from these prepositions: from, in, to, with, for, of. *You may use them more than once.*

EXAMPLE WRITING

3 Abraham Lincoln was the sixteenth president _____ the United States. He was

elected president _____ 1860 during a controversial and heated period of American

history. As more states applied _____ membership in the growing country, the issue

_____ slavery kept surfacing. There was an unstable balance _____ slave states

and free states. Each time another state was added _____ the Union, the balance of

power shifted. Lincoln was _____ a free state, and many _____ the slave state

leaders viewed Lincoln as an enemy of their cause _____ expand slavery. _____

the end, no compromise could be reached, and the slave states seceded _____ the

U.S. in order to form their own independent country. Hostilities grew, and _____

1861 the Civil War, or the War Between the States as it is sometimes called, broke out.

During the next four years, the Civil War ravaged the country. By the end of the war in

1865, the American countryside was _____ shambles, but the union was once again

intact. Through his military and political decisions, Lincoln is credited _____ saving

the country _____ self-destruction.

Practice 4   *Editing for Errors*

There are eight errors in this paragraph. They are in word forms (1), articles (2), modals (1), verb tense (2), and subject-verb agreement (2). Mark these errors and write corrections.

EXAMPLE WRITING

4   Washington and Lincoln was similarly in several ways. Both men are U.S. presidents. Both men served the United States during extremely difficult times. For Washington, the question is whether the United States would be able to maintain its independence from Britain. The United States was certainly very fragile nation at that time. For Lincoln, the question were really not so different. Would the United States to be able to survive during what was one of darkest periods of American history?

Practice 5   *Sentence Fragments*

After you read this paragraph, find the three sentence fragments. Correct the fragments by (1) changing the punctuation and creating one complete sentence, or (2) adding new words to make the fragment a complete sentence.

EXAMPLE WRITING

5   There were also several differences between Washington and Lincoln. Washington came from a wealthy aristocratic background. He had several years of schooling. Lincoln came from a poor background and he had very little schooling. Another difference between the two involved their military roles. Washington was a general. He was a military leader. Became president. Lincoln never served in the military. He was a lawyer who early on became a politician. When he became president, he took on the role of commander in chief, as all U.S. presidents do. Despite his lack of military background or training. Lincoln made several strategic decisions that enabled the U.S. military leaders to win the Civil War. Finally, Washington served for two terms and therefore had eight years to accomplish his policies. Lincoln, on the other hand, was assassinated. While in office and was not able to finish some of the things that he wanted for the country.

Practice 6   *Editing for Errors*

There are seven errors in this paragraph. They are in articles (2), verb tense (1), inappropriate words (1), word forms (1), number (singular and plural) (1), and subject-verb agreement (1). Mark these errors and make corrections.

EXAMPLE WRITING

6   The names George Washington and Abraham Lincoln is known even to people who have never been to the United States. Both of these patriots gave large part of their lives to help America make what it is today though they served the country in very different ways in complete different time in the American history. Though they were gone, their legacies and contributions continue to affect us.

Appendix 3

Connectors

Using connectors will help your ideas flow. Remember that when connectors occur at the beginning of a sentence, they are often followed by a comma.

Purpose	Conjunctions between independent clauses	Conjunctions that begin dependent clauses	Transitions (usually precede independent clauses)
examples			For example, To illustrate, Specifically, In particular,
information	and		In addition, Moreover, Furthermore,
comparison			Similarly, Likewise, In the same way,
contrast	but	while although	In contrast, However, On the other hand, Conversely, Instead,
refutation			On the contrary,
concession	yet	although though even though it may appear that	Nevertheless, Even so, Admittedly, Despite this,
emphasis			In fact, Actually,

Purpose	Conjunctions between independent clauses	Conjunctions that begin dependent clauses	Transitions (usually precede independent clauses)
clarification			In other words, In simpler words, More simply,
reason or cause	for	because since	
result	so	so so that	As a result, As a consequence, Consequently, Therefore, Thus,
time relationships		after as soon as before when while until whenever as	afterward first second next then finally subsequently meanwhile in the meantime
condition		if even if unless provided that when	
purpose		so that in order that	
choice	or		
conclusion			In conclusion, To summarize, As we have seen, In brief, In closing, To sum up, Finally,

Appendix 4

Peer Editing Sheets

**UNIT 2, Activity 11, page 62
Narrative Essay Outline**

Writer: _____ Date: _____

Peer editor: _____

Topic: _____

1. Is the hook interesting? _____ If not, how could it be made more interesting?

   _____

2. How many paragraphs are going to be in the essay? _____

3. What action or event does each topic sentence show?

   Paragraph 1: _____

   Paragraph 2: _____

   Paragraph 3: _____

   Paragraph 4: _____

   Paragraph 5: _____

4. Is there a good ending to the action of the story? _____ If not, can you

   suggest a change to the ending?

5. What kind of ending will the story have, a moral or a revelation/prediction?

   _____

6. Do you think this essay will have enough information? Does the story leave out anything important?

   Write suggestions here. _____

   _____

7. The best part of the outline is _____

_____

8. Questions I still have about the outline are _____

_____

**UNIT 2, Activity 13, page 63
Narrative Essay**

Writer: _____ Date: _____

Peer editor: _____

Essay title: _____

1. What are the three most memorable details in the essay? (Don't look back at the essay.)

    a. _____

    b. _____

    c. _____

2. Identify the hook. Is it effective? _____ Make any suggestions here.

   _____

3. What is the main point or thesis? _____

   _____

4. Reread the essay and underline all the connectors that you can find. Does the writer use them correctly? Circle any connectors that are incorrect.

5. Is the story in chronological order? _____ If necessary, make any suggestions for

   changes about the order of events. _____

   _____

6. Does the essay have sentence variety? _____ If not, mark the sentences that could be

   varied or make some suggestions for sentence variety. _____

   _____

7. What verb tense does the writer mainly use? _____ Is this tense used throughout the

essay? _____ If not, are the different tenses necessary or should they be changed?

Use a highlighter to mark all unnecessary changes in tense.

8. Does the conclusion effectively end the action? _____ If not, write a few suggestions

for a better ending. _____

_____

UNIT 3, Activity 8, p. 85
Comparison Essay Outline

Writer: _____ Date: _____

Peer editor: _____

Topic: _____

1. Is the thesis statement clear? _____ If not, make suggestions for changes.

   _____

2. Does the writer use the block or the point-by-point method of organization? _____

   Is this method effective for the subject? _____ If not, make suggestions for changes.

   _____

3. Does each topic sentence clearly state the point of comparison? _____ If not, make

   suggestions for improvement. _____

   _____

4. Do these two subjects have enough similarities and/or differences for a good comparison essay?

   _____ If not, why not? _____

   _____

5. The best part of the outline is _____

   _____

6. Questions I still have about the outline are _____

   _____

PEER EDITING SHEET #4   **UNIT 3, Activity 10, p. 85**
Comparison Essay

Writer: _____ Date: _____

Peer editor: _____

Essay title: _____

1. In a few words, what is the essay about? _____

   _____

2. Identify the hook. Is it effective? _____ Make any suggestions here.

   _____

3. Does each body paragraph contain a clear topic sentence? _____ If not, underline any

   sections that need improvement.

4. What method of organization does the writer use? _____ List the main points that

   the writer compares. _____

   _____

5. Are the comparisons supported with examples? (Ask *who? what? where? when? why? how?*)

   _____ If not, put a star (*) next to the places that need supporting information.

6. Does the writer use connectors correctly? _____ If not, circle any incorrect connec-

   tors or any places that need connectors.

7. Does the writer restate the thesis in the conclusion? _____ If not, bring this to the

   attention of the writer.

8. In the conclusion, does the writer offer an opinion or a suggestion about the two subjects?

_____ Do you agree with the writer's final words? _____ If not, why not?

_____

PEER EDITING SHEET #5   **UNIT 4, Activity 10, p. 103**
                          Cause-Effect Essay Outline

Writer: _____ Date: _____

Peer editor: _____

Topic: _____

1. What kind of essay will this be, cause or effect? _____ Can you tell this from the the-

   sis statement? _____ If not, what changes can you suggest to make the purpose of the

   essay clearer? _____

   _____

2. Read the topic sentence for each body paragraph. Is it related to the thesis? If not, mark the topic
   sentences that need more work.

3. Do the supporting details relate to the topic sentences? _____ If not, which para-

   graph(s) need to be developed further? _____

4. The best part of the outline is _____

   _____

5. Questions I still have about the outline are _____

   _____

UNIT 4, Activity 12, p. 104
Cause-Effect Essay

Writer: _____ Date: _____

Peer editor: _____

Essay title: _____

1. In a few words, what is the essay about? _____

   _____

2. Reread the introductory paragraph. Do the ideas progress smoothly from the hook to the thesis

   statement? _____ If not, what suggestions for changes would you make to the writer?

   _____

   _____

3. Do all the topic sentences support the thesis statement? _____ Mark any that do not

   and write the reason. _____

   _____

   _____

4. Look at the supporting details in each paragraph. Are they related to the topic sentence? If not,
   underline the details that need revision.

5. Check the connectors in the essay. Is it easy to understand the connection between the causes

   and effects? If not, what is missing or needs to be changed? _____

   _____

6. As you reread the essay, check for wordiness. Circle any that you find and, if you want, suggest a
   way to eliminate the wordiness.

7. Does the writer restate the thesis in the conclusion? _____ If not, bring this to the attention of the writer.

8. Compare the introduction and conclusion paragraphs. Can you see logical connections between the two? _____ If not, why not? What suggestions for improvement can you make?

_____

_____

UNIT 5, Activity 9, p. 122
Argumentative Essay Outline

Writer: _____ Date: _____

Peer editor: _____

Topic: _____

    If the answer to any of these questions is "no," tell the writer why and make any suggestions for improvement that you can think of.

    1. Is the hook interesting (does it catch the reader's attention)?   Yes   No

    2. Is the writer's opinion clear in the thesis statement?   Yes   No

    3. Do the topic sentences in the body paragraphs support the thesis?   Yes   No

    4. In each paragraph, do the supporting details relate to the topic sentence?   Yes   No

    5. Are the counterargument and refutation strong?   Yes   No

       Do they make sense?   Yes   No

    6. Does the writer restate the thesis in the conclusion?   Yes   No

    7. The best part of the outline is _____

    _____

    8. Questions I still have about the outline are _____

    _____

UNIT 5, Activity 11, p. 122
Argumentative Essay

Writer: _____ Date: _____

Peer editor: _____

Essay title: _____

1. In a few words, what is the essay about? _____

   _____

2. Reread the introductory paragraph. Do the ideas progress smoothly from the hook to the thesis

   statement? _____ If not, what suggestions for changes would you make to the writer?

   _____

   _____

3. Do all the topic sentences support the thesis statement? _____ Mark any that do not

   and write the reason. _____

   _____

   _____

4. Look at the supporting details in each paragraph. Are they related to the topic sentence? If not,
   underline the details that need revision.

5. Underline any modals. Are *must*, *had better*, or *should* used correctly to assert a point? Are *may*,
   might, *could*, *can*, or *would* used correctly to acknowledge an opposing opinion? Make suggestions
   for changes where necessary.

6. Reread the essay and look for any faulty logic. If you find any, write it here and suggest a way to

   eliminate the faulty logic. _____

_____

_____

7. Find the paragraph that contains the counterargument and refutation. Is the counterargument

   stated clearly? _____ Is the refutation strong? _____ Does it make another

   point in support of the writer's argument? _____ If necessary, suggest changes to the

   writer to make the counterargument and refutation more effective.

8. Is the conclusion effective, that is, does it restate the thesis and the writer's opinion?

   _____ If not, how can the conclusion be improved?

   _____

Appendix 5

Answer Key

UNIT 1

Activity 1, pp. 5–9

3. Ironing clothes, washing dishes, and cleaning the bathroom

4. Hook: "Everyone knows how the story of Cinderella ends, but did you ever think about how she spent her days before she met the prince?"

5. Answers will vary.

6. 5 paragraphs; paragraph 1 (introduction); paragraph 5 (conclusion); paragraphs 2, 3, 4 (body)

7. Unpleasant household chores

8. "The top three of these tasks include ironing clothes, washing dishes, and cleaning the bathroom."

9. Ironing clothes; "One of the most hated chores for many people is ironing clothes because it is not a task that can be completed quickly or thoughtlessly."

10. Paragraph 3: "Another household chore that many people dislike is washing dishes." Paragraph 4: "Though ironing clothes and washing dishes are not the most pleasant household chores, perhaps the most dreaded is cleaning the bathroom."

11. Two possible supporting sentences: "Each piece of clothing must be handled individually, so a basket of laundry can take hours!" "If you do not follow these directions carefully, it might become wrinkled and you have to start over."

12. "Because the bathroom is full of germs, a quick wiping of the surfaces is not enough."

13. "Maintaining a house means doing a wide variety of unpleasant chores."

Activity 2, pp. 10–12

3. Answers will vary.

4. Hook: "What would happen if you woke up one day and suddenly found yourself in a world where you could not communicate with anyone?"

5. Answers will vary.

6. 7 paragraphs; paragraph 6

7. The author did not realize that the word *flour* had been misunderstood as *flower*.

8. (1) The writer studied Japanese. (2) The writer arrived in Japan. (3) The writer wanted to make some bread. (4) The writer went to the store. (5) The writer looked all over the store for the flour. (6) The writer saw one of his students. (7) The writer asked the student for a Japanese translation. (8) The writer spoke to an elderly clerk. (9) The clerk took the writer to the produce section. (10) The clerk pointed to the flowers. (11) The writer realized that the student had not understood the question correctly. (12) The writer went home without the flour.

Activity 3, pp. 13–15

3. Topic: differences in urban life and rural life

4. Thesis: "Perhaps some of the most notable differences in the lives of these two groups include degree of friendliness, pace of life, and variety of activities."

5. Urban

6. Activities: paragraph 4; more options for activities: city

7. Pace (paragraph 3): *urban:* **1.** In the city, life moves very quickly. **2.** The streets reflect this hectic place and are rarely empty, even late at night. **3.** City dwellers appear to be racing to get somewhere important. **4.** Life for them tends to be a series of deadlines. *rural:* **1.** In the country, life is much slower. **2.** Even during peak hours, traffic jams occur less often. **3.** Stores close in the early evening, and the streets don't come alive until the next morning. **4.** The people here seem more relaxed and move in a more leisurely way.

Activity 4, pp. 16–18

3. Some cancer can be prevented by lifestyle changes.

4. Cancer is related to certain behaviors.

5. Thesis: "By eating better, exercising regularly, and staying out of the sun, people can reduce their risks."

6. The body paragraphs will discuss (1) eating better, (2) exercising regularly, (3) staying out of the sun.

7. "These common foods contain large amounts of saturated fat, which is the worst kind of fat." "However, eating fatty foods can increase a person's chances for some kinds of cancer. Lack of fiber in a person's diet can increase the chance of colon cancer."

8. ". . . many people still buy food that contains fat because it often tastes better."

Activity 5, pp. 18–22

3. Community colleges and universities; community colleges

4. Thesis statement: "However, if the choice is based on three specific factors, namely, cost, location, and quality of education, students will quickly see the advantages that attending a community college offers."

Paragraph 2 topic: Costs

A. Community college cost: less than $3,000

B. University cost: almost $5,000

C. Other costs: 2. Photocopying costs; 3. Cafeteria prices; 5. Textbook prices

Paragraph 3:

B. Parents' reasons

Paragraph 4 topic: Educational benefits

B. Library facilities

5–9. Answers will vary.

Activity 6, pp. 26–28

1. Hooks 1–3. Answers will vary.

2. Answers will vary.

Activity 7, pp. 28–29

1. Thesis: "I object to mandatory retirement for capable workers because it violates personal choice, discriminates against senior citizens, and wastes valuable skills as well as money."

2. Direct—It gives the three reasons that will be discussed.

3. Answers will vary. Sample indirect thesis statement: "Capable workers should not be forced to retire when they reach a certain age."

Activity 8, pp. 29–30

1. Hooks 1–3. Answers will vary.

2. Answers will vary.

Activity 9, pp. 30–33

1. Thesis: "However, in the area of education, there are several notable differences between South Korea on the one hand and Canada and the United States on the other."

2. Indirect—a statement of the discussion topic only

3. Answers will vary. Sample direct thesis statement: "Education in South Korea, on one hand, and in the United States and Canada, on the other hand, are different in the hours of study, society's attitude toward education, and scholarships."

Activity 10, pp. 33–34

Title: "How Do You Say . . . ?"

    I. C. Thesis statement: "One event in particular stands out as an example of my inability to express my ideas to the people around me due to my lack of vocabulary."

    II. A. Paragraph 2 topic sentence: "I wanted to make some fresh bread, so I set out for the store with the simple intention of buying some flour."

    B. Paragraph 3 topic sentence: "I wandered around the store a few times, but I did not see a bag of anything that appeared to be flour."

    C. Paragraph 4 topic sentence: "I desperately wanted to ask one of the three elderly women clerks where the flour was, but I could not do this simple task."

    D. Paragraph 5 topic sentence: "I rushed back into the store, which was about to close for the evening."

Activity 11, pp. 34–36

    I. A. Hook: "Everyone knows how the story of Cinderella ends, but did you ever think about how she spent her days before she met the prince?"

    B. Connecting information: "Her daily routine was not glamorous. She did everything from sweeping the floors to cooking the meals. If someone had asked Cinderella, 'Are there any household chores that you particularly hate?' she probably would have answered, 'Why, none, of course. Housework is my duty!' In the real world, however, most people have definite dislikes for certain household chores."

    C. Thesis statement: "The top three of these tasks include ironing clothes, washing dishes, and cleaning the bathroom."

    II. A. Topic sentence (chore #1): "One of the most hated choices for many people is ironing clothes because it is not a task that can be completed quickly or thoughtlessly."

        a. (3) "Getting the creases just right."

           (4) "Placing it on a hanger."

        b. Problem: "If it becomes wrinkled, you have to start over."

    B. Topic sentence (chore #2): "Another household chore that many people dislike is washing dishes."

           b. (2) "Patience"

              (3) "Must be done every day"

    C. 1. Topic sentence (chore #3): "Though ironing clothes and washing dishes are not the most pleasant household chores, perhaps the most dreaded is cleaning the bathroom."

   2. a. (1) Cleaning the bathtub

      b. (2) "Must use strong bathroom cleansers"

      c. Positive aspect: "It doesn't have to be cleaned daily."

Activity 12, p. 38

Answers will vary.

UNIT 2

Activity 1, pp. 40–41

X sentences: (5) Whales are by far the largest marine mammals. (6) She gave her
    friend a birthday gift. (8) The Russian dictionary that we use in our language
    class has 500 pages.

Activity 2, pp. 43–47

  3. Narrative hook: "I had never been more anxious in my life."

  4. Answers will vary.

  5. At an airport

  6. Theme: A difficult and confusing experience at the airport ends well.

  7. Mood: frustration

  8. Characters: narrator, passing businessman, airport employee

  9. Past tense; *five sample verbs:* tried, came, arrived, dragged, watched

 10. Yes; *first:* watched bus driver set luggage on sidewalk; *second:* could not make
     sense of signs; *third:* tried to ask businessman for help; *fourth:* followed a group
     to elevator; *fifth:* airport employee helped

 11. Transitional sentences: (paragraph 2) "I had to find help because I couldn't be
     late!" (paragraph 3) "I could follow them to the right place and I wouldn't have
     to say a word to them." (paragraph 4) "A high squeaking noise announced the
     opening of the doors, and I looked around <u>timidly</u>." (paragraph 5) "He led me
     past all the lines of people and pushed my luggage to the inspection counter."

 12. Revelation: "He helped me when I needed it the most. I can only hope that
     one day I will be able to do the same for another traveler who is suffering
     through a terrible journey."

Activity 3, pp. 47–49

Title: "Frustration at the Airport"

    I. B. Connecting information: "I had just spent the last three endless hours try-
       ing to get to the airport so that I could travel home."

      C. Thesis statement: "Now, as I watched the bus driver set my luggage on the
       airport sidewalk, I realized that my frustration had only just begun."

II. A. 3. Transition sentence: "I had to find help because I couldn't be late!"

    B. Paragraph 3 topic sentence (event 2): "I tried to ask a passing businessman for help, but all my words came out wrong."

      3. "Another bus arrived."

      4. Transition sentence: "I could follow them to the right place and I wouldn't have to say a word to them."

    C. 1. "They all fit in, but there wasn't enough room for me."

      3. "I pressed button 3. The elevator slowly climbed up to the third floor and jerked to a stop."

      4. Transition sentence: "A high squeaking noise announced the opening of the doors, and I looked around timidly."

    D. 2. "He gave me his handkerchief."

      3. "He led me down a long hallway."

III. A. Close of the action: "When I turned to thank him for all his help, he was gone."

    C. "He helped me when I needed it the most."

    D. Final sentence (prediction or revelation): "I can only hope that one day I will be able to do the same for another traveler who is suffering through a terrible journey.

Activity 4, pp. 49–50

Answers will vary.

Activity 5, pp. 51–53

Some answers may vary. Sample answers: (paragraph 1) Now; (paragraph 2) While, When; (paragraph 3) As soon as, Next, Then; (paragraph 4) after, until; (paragraph 5) First, Then, Finally

Activity 6, pp. 54–55

a. When I looked down at it, the hill was steep and scary.

b. After I built up some speed on my trip toward the edge, I suddenly got scared.

c. As soon as my mother rushed over to me, she put her hands on my shoulders and began talking to me.

d. When she gave me a cookie, she scolded me for being so reckless.

Activity 7, p. 56

1. Your last day in high school

2. A scary airplane ride to another city

3. Buying your first car

    4. Your brother's embarrassing wedding ceremony

    5. What I did last New Year's Eve.

Activities 8–14, pp. 57–63

Answers will vary.

UNIT 3

Activity 1, pp. 67–70

    3. Brazil and the United States

    4. Point-by-point

    5. Hook: All countries in the world are unique.

    6. Thesis: "On the contrary, they share many similarities." Restated thesis (paragraph 5): "Although Brazil and the United States are unique countries, there are significant similarities in their size, ethnic groups, and personal values."

    7. Size: *Brazil:* "Brazil covers almost half of the South American continent. Few Brazilians can say that they have traveled extensively within its borders. Because of Brazil's large size, its weather varies greatly from one area to another." *United States:* "Like Brazil, the United States takes up a significant portion of its continent (North America), so most Americans have visited only a few of the fifty states. In addition, the United States has a wide range of climates."

    8. Opinion: "Nevertheless, it is important to remember that people as a whole have more in common than they generally think they do."

Activity 2, pp. 70–72

Title: Not As Different As You Think

  I. C. Thesis statement: "On the contrary, they have many similarities."

  II. A. Paragraph 2 (similarity 1) topic sentence: One important similarity is their size.

      1. Brazil's characteristics

        a. Size: Brazil covers almost half of the South American continent.

        c. Climate: Because of Brazil's large size, its weather varies greatly from one area to another.

      2. United States' characteristics

        a. Size: Like Brazil, the United States takes up a significant portion of its continent (North America).

        b. Travel: Most Americans have visited only a few of the fifty states.

B. 1. a. Europe

         c. Native people

    2. d. Asia

         e. South America

C. Paragraph 4 (similarity 3) topic sentence: "Finally, individualism is an important value for both Brazilians and Americans."

    1. Brazilians' belief in freedom: means that they have the right to do and be whatever they desire as long as they don't hurt others

    2. American's belief in freedom: Individualism and freedom of choice also exist in the United States, where freedom is perhaps the highest value of the people.

III. A. Restated thesis: "Although Brazil and the United States are unique countries, there are remarkable similarities in their size, ethnic groups, and personal values."

Activity 3, pp. 72–74

Answers will vary.

Activity 4, pp. 75–77

(paragraph 1) However; (paragraph 2) However, Unlike; (paragraph 3) In addition, In contrast; (paragraph 4) Even though, On the other hand; (paragraph 5) Although

Activity 5, pp. 80–81

Answers may vary. Sample answers:

3. Yes. Compare classes, teachers, study time
4. No. Change "tourist attractions in Toronto" to "the weather in Vancouver"
5. Yes. Compare kinds, life, food
6. No. Change to: "Macintosh/IBM-compatible computer"
7. No. Change to: "hands/feet of chimpanzees and humans"
8. Yes. Compare features
9. No. Change "the Earth" to "South American continent"
10. Yes. Compare ingredients, taste, price

Activities 6–11, pp. 81–85

Answers will vary.

UNIT 4

Activity 1, pp. 87–89

3. Thesis: The fact is that we lie for many reasons.

4. Pinocchio, the boy who cried wolf, George Washington

5. The white lie and the protective lie

6. Opinion: "We never know when our lies might be exposed and cause us embarrassment or the loss of people's trust."

Activity 2, pp. 90–92

Answers will vary. Sample answers:

Focus-on-cause outline

    I. (Thesis statement): ". . . low self-esteem, lack of parental guidance, and peer pressure.

   II. A. (Paragraph 2) 3. Drugs may help teens escape the reality of their lives.

      B. (Paragraph 3) topic sentence: Teens who use drugs often suffer a lack of parental guidance.

      C. (Paragraph 4) topic sentence: Many teens use drugs because of peer pressure.

  III. (Restated thesis): Low self-esteem, lack of parental guidance, and peer pressure are three of the causes behind much teenage drug use.

Focus-on-effect outline

   II. A. (Paragraph 2) 3. They may become violent.

      B. (Paragraph 3) topic sentence: Drug use often has a negative effect on academic performance.

      C. (Paragraph 4) 3. Some teens will take dangerous risks to get money for drugs.

  III. (Restated thesis): A teenager's drug use can ruin family relationships, academic performance, and social behavior.

Activity 3, pp. 93–94

Answers will vary.

Activity 4, pp. 95–97

(paragraph 1) Because of; (paragraph 2) As the result of, For this reason; (paragraph 3) Consequently; (paragraph 4) As a result, Because of, As a result of; (paragraph 5) Because of

Activity 5, p. 98

Wordiness: considered, the purpose of, made statements saying, for all intents and purposes, despite the fact that, when all is said and done, contents of the

Activity 6, p. 99

Possible redundant information: on TV or at the movies; future; planets and galaxies; without the exchange of words in these futuristic programs; who can read minds and know the innermost thoughts and secrets of other people; untrue; everyday

Activities 7–13, pp. 100–104

Answers will vary.

UNIT 5

Activity 1, pp. 106–109

3. Individualism is a fundamental value in the United States.

4. School uniforms are the better choice for three reasons.

5. *paragraph 2:* First, wearing school uniforms would help make students' lives simpler. *paragraph 3:* Second, school uniforms influence students to act responsibly in groups and as individuals. *paragraph 4:* Finally, school uniforms would help make all the students feel equal.

6. Implementing mandatory school uniforms would make all the students look the same regardless of their financial status.

7. Paragraph 5. Opponents of mandatory uniforms say that students who wear school uniforms cannot express their individuality.

8. . . . school is a place to learn, not to <u>flaunt</u> wealth and fashion.

9. In conclusion, there are many well-documented benefits to implementing mandatory school uniforms for students.

10. Public schools should require uniforms in order to benefit both the students and society as a whole.

Activity 2, pp. 111–112

Answers will vary.

Activity 3, pp. 113–114

Answers will vary.

Activity 4, pp. 115–116

(paragraph 1) will; (paragraph 2) should, ought to; (paragraph 3) shouldn't, has to; (paragraph 4) should, must; (paragraph 5) might; (paragraph 6) should, ought to, can

Activity 5, pp. 116–117

Answers will vary.

Activity 6, p. 119

"fine upstanding citizens" (loaded words)

"apathetic leaders" (loaded words)

"run happily" (loaded words)

"Last year that city raised its sales tax by 1 percent. Only three weeks later, the city was nearly destroyed by a riot in the streets." (events related only by sequence)

"If we want to keep our fair city as it is, we must either vote NO on the ballot question or live in fear of violence." (either/or argument)

Activities 7–12, pp. 120–123

Answers will vary.

APPENDIX 2

Essay 22

Practice 1, page 135

corrections: offers, keep, are, travel

Practice 2, page 136

take, entering, sit, sleep, give, done, is given, give, waits, turns

Practice 3, pages 136–137

In addition; Even if; For example; but; First; Because

Practice 4, page 137

Blanks that require articles: <u>the</u> important; <u>the</u> (<u>a</u>) Japanese; <u>a</u> problem; <u>the</u> goal; <u>the</u> concept; <u>a</u> great

Practice 5, page 138

In, with, to, into, of, about, in, around, in

Essay 23

Practice 1, pages 138–139

do, calls, were, was, was, talking, shouted, slapped, was, teach, be, succeed, is, be used

Practice 2, page 139

of, for, of, of in, in, in, of

Practice 3, pages 139–140

Blanks that require articles: <u>an</u> ineffective, <u>a</u> child, <u>a</u> long-term, <u>a</u> mild, <u>the</u> (<u>a</u>) standard

Practice 4, page 140

Answers may vary. Sample answers:

Furthermore, it increases disruptive behavior that can become more <u>aggressive. This</u> leads to school violence and bullying of fellow students.

Supporters of corporal punishment believe that it is necessary to maintain a good learning environment, <u>but</u> it is unfortunate that the opposite result often happens.

Practice 5, pages 140–141

are spanked; to use; show; were; contributes; has found; were observed; punish

Practice 6, pages 141–142

(fragment) Therefore, we should consider alternatives to corporal <u>punishment because</u> discipline is necessary to educate children.

(subject-verb agreement) One of the alternatives ~~are~~ is

(subject-verb agreement) ~~is~~ are the most powerful motivators

(article) for ~~the~~ learning

(word form) ~~behave~~ behavior

(word form) punish~~ment~~

(verb tense) ~~taught~~ teach

Practice 7, page 142

(articles) In ~~the~~ conclusion

(subject-verb agreement) Discipline and love ~~is~~ are

(comma splice) is not opposites, <u>so</u> (or, <u>and</u>) punishment

(articles) letting ~~the~~ children

(articles) beat ~~a~~ student

(word forms) with the hope~~ful~~

(sentence fragment) more humane <u>alternatives in</u> order to

Essay 24

Practice 1, pages 142–143

<u>the</u> United States; <u>the</u> same country; <u>the</u> country

Practice 2, page 143

knows; appreciate; is; was; helping; beaten; become

Practice 3, page 144

of; in; for; of; of; to; from; of; to; In; from; in; in; with; from

Practice 4, pages 144–145

(subject-verb agreement) Washington and Lincoln ~~was~~ were

(word form) similar~~ly~~

(verb tense) Both men ~~are~~ were

(verb tense) the question ~~is~~ was

(article) certainly <u>a</u> very fragile

(subject-verb agreement) the question ~~were~~ was

(modal) Would the United States ~~to~~ be able to

(article) one of <u>the</u> darkest periods

Practice 5, page 145

(1) He was a military <u>leader who became</u> president.

(2) Despite his lack of military background or <u>training, Lincoln</u> made several strategic decisions that enabled the U.S. military leaders to win the Civil War.

(3) Lincoln, on the other hand, was <u>assassinated while</u> in office and was not able to finish some of the things that he wanted for the country.

Practice 6, page 146

(subject-verb agreement) names George Washington and Abraham Lincoln ~~is~~ are known

(article) gave <u>a</u> large part

(inappropriate word) to help America ~~make~~ become

(word form) in complete<u>ly</u>

(number) time<u>s</u>

(article) in ~~the~~ American history

(verb tense) Though they ~~were~~ are gone,